MODERN PHOBIAS

Modern Phobias

A Litany of Contemporary Fears

Tim Lihoreau

BLOOMSBURY

First published in Great Britain in 2006

Copyright © 2006 by Tim Lihoreau

Drawings copyright © 2006 by Jim Smith
Email Jim Smith at www.waldopancake.com

The moral right of the author has been asserted

Bloomsbury Publishing Plc, 36 Soho Square, London W1D 3QY

www.bloomsbury.com

Bloomsbury Publishing, London, New York and Berlin

A CIP catalogue record for this book is
available from the British Library

ISBN 0 7475 8398 6
ISBN-13 9780747583981

10 9 8 7 6 5 4 3 2 1

Typeset by Palimpsest Book Production Ltd,
Grangemouth, Stirlingshire
Printed in Great Britain by Clays Ltd, St Ives plc

All papers used by Bloomsbury Publishing are natural,
recyclable products made from wood grown in well-managed
forests. The manufacturing processes conform to the
environmental regulations of the country of origin

For Siobhan, for enduring and accepting my phobias these last fifteen years

Fronsophobia was the first to strike.

I remember the occasion vividly. It was Christmas 1977, and the last vestiges of silvery jubilation were being wrung out of a particularly halcyon year. Looking back on it now, life showed every sign of simply getting better and better, until what should have been a golden Christmas morning suddenly turned cold with fear. After moistened kisses had been parried and traditional Irish coffee sunk, I was charged with making tea for three aunts, one uncle, two neighbours, parents and assorted hangers-on. A manageable group to some, perhaps, but in no time I was gripped by fronsophobia. I was never the same again. In my late teens I realised that I was also agmenophobic, but it was only when acute versurphobia kicked in, in my twenties, that I decided to make it my month's work to collate a reference book of these truly disabling fears. Of course, some of the phobias herein work very much *for* the patient – the so-called 'friendly fears'. Psychologists now believe these are the body's way of helping the sufferer avoid *ludificorus ipsus totus*, or making a complete arse of oneself. (By way of example, see rusmusophobia, fear of country music.) Where possible I have tried to give the reader further reading material, albeit totally fictitious, and on occasion I've attempted to give solace to sufferers by pointing out any famous patients. Chronic nimitempophobia prevents me from saying any more.

Tim Lihoreau
2006

foreword by a fake doctor

Being A Fake Doctor, I am often asked, 'Fake Doctor, are the *Modern Phobias* in this book real?' Of course, my answer is invariably variable: 'Yes and no. That is to say, perhaps, but maybe not.' You see, I think it possible that there is not a single person to whom at least one of these *Modern Phobias*, somewhere in this book, does not apply. For example, who can honestly say they have not, at some time in their life, felt a creeping feeling that something may not be quite right as they approach the cash point towards the end of the month? (See arcaphobia.) Which man amongst us can put his hand on his pants and say that his eyes have never widened due to the first stirrings that lead to subturrophobia? Even I, with all my years of fake medical experience, have been known to treat certain imaginary patients differently due to my illenomophobic tendencies.

In public life, too, I fear there are many folk suffering from all manner of *Modern Phobias*. Many of Stephen Fry's friends, for example, have openly admitted to being aliacallophobes. Lourdes Ciccone is said to be a paremusophobe. Thankfully, though, some celebrities do manage to overcome their fears – George Michael is certainly no longer a forlatriphobe.

In everyday life, however, there are still taboos surrounding many of these fears. Very few people will acknowledge that they are abcellophobic or amipartophobic, and yet fake doctors estimate that one in five of the population are chronic sufferers; most UK males are either bulliphobic or illerogophobic, or both; and in our working lives, antefamaphobia is thought to account for many thousands of lost man hours. The figure rises to millions in politics.

As with most afflicted folk, sufferers of *Modern Phobias* deserve nothing if not your sympathy.

A Fake Doctor
August 2006

abcellophobia
fear of leaving a toilet cubicle

Forced underground in the Victorian era – largely due to Queen Victoria's refusal to acknowledge that toilets existed – only the 'swinging sixties' (with flower power) and the 'sad seventies' (with Toilet Duck) enabled **abcellophobia** to break free from its taboo. Contemporary **abcellophobes** usually find symptoms occur when, already *en compartement*, they hear their boss enter. A 'raging desire for anonymity' (as one sufferer puts it) sees them prepared to remain in the cubicle for as long as it takes their path to clear. For many, the fear of having to own up to the vile stench keeps them there. If they are lucky enough to escape the loo but meet their boss outside, some feel the need to make endless small talk rather than emit the career-damaging line, 'I'd give it ten minutes.'

1

Many sufferers have reported the inverse phobia, whereby they will not even enter a cubicle if their boss is already in the toilet (*abcellophobia strictus cultus*), preferring to pretend they came in merely to wash their hands. Doctors also think that *abcellophobia adlevia* is related, the main symptom of which is the patient's refusal to enter a lift for fear of having to make conversation with a boss (its inverse being *abcellophobia nasus fulvus*). See also **detrimenophobia**.

[orig. der.: *ab*, away from; *cellula*, little room; *strictus*, tight; *cultus*, buttocks; *adlevia*, lifting; *nasus*, nose; *fulvus*, brown]

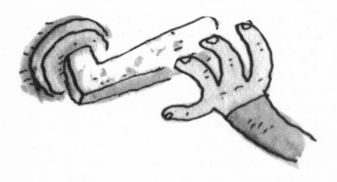

abemoraphobia
fear of having missed one's stop

The fleeting nature of **abemoraphobia** leads some doctors to place it dismissively in the same dubious medical category as acupuncture, long-term back-ache and the acting in *Holby City*. A minority of sufferers have *abemoraphobia interdiu*, which causes a queasy welling-up in the stomach and, occasionally, a panic-fuelled mad dash to the train/bus door. Far more common is *abemoraphobia nocturnia*, which afflicts already fatigued travellers eager for sleep on late trains. Victims of *a.n.* suffer from a malfunctioning of the internal body clock, which appears to press its own 'snooze' button. Thus the *a.n.* sufferer will wake up with a snort just after the train has pulled into each station, then make a Jacques Tati-esque, windmill lunge for their briefcase before realising it is not their stop. They will continue to do this every seven minutes or so, as the train pulls into each succes-sive station. In 90 per cent of cases, faulty body clocks seem to repair themselves just before the sufferer's intended stop, enabling them to get some much-needed sleep. All the way to the terminus.

[orig. der.: *aberrare*, to go astray; *mora*, delay; *interdiu*, by day; *nocturnus*, by night]

aedificatorphobia
fear of builders

Like **rusmusophobia** (q.v.) and **vendomophobia** (q.v.), **aedificatorphobia** is erroneously thought to be one of the friendly fears, on the grounds that, if you fear your builders, you must be quite sane. Whatever the ins and out of it, doctors say **aedificatorphobia** is definitely on the increase. Most sufferers fail to realise they have the phobia until too late. They think they are immune, that their builder is more of a friend (and it's just a coincidence that his name is Jerry). He was able to quote them for virtually everything they wanted done. Turns out his firm not only does the structural building work; it also does tiling, plastering, repointing, landscape gardening, re-turfing, fencing, quantity surveying, pest control, getting stones out of horses' hooves and solving global warming. Everything. How lucky you were to find them. Of course, that's when the Herbert Lom twitch begins to develop. Symptoms? Well, symptoms include a tendency to live amongst rubble, to communicate via a third party and, sadly, the ability to sit through the 'O' Reilly Builders' episode of *Fawlty Towers* without laughing once.

[orig. der.: *aedificator*, builder]

aestaphobia
fear of summer

To anyone smaller than a size 16 (women) or 36 waist (men), the whole concept of **aestaphobia** must be alien. For them, summer is eagerly anticipated, longed for even. Global warming? It's a good thing, surely. Well, for an **aestaphobe,** summer is akin to a tenth level of hell which Dante forgot to write up. Sufferers divide into two groups: those with *aestaphobia titubens* and those with *aestaphobia astacus. Titubens* (derived from the Latin 'to wobble') patients feel a little overweight and fear the traditions of summer: the fanning of newspapers on trains, the need for light, unflattering clothes and sweat patches under the arms. *Astacus* (meaning lobster) sufferers are all too aware of the fact that, rather than taking on a classic bronze, their skin turns either a glowing, overdone pink or, occasionally, a virulent 'Dickinson orange', which, although enabling them to blend in unseen aside an easyJet plane, means nevertheless that they prefer to spend their summers in Lapland.

[orig. der.: *aesta*, summer]

agmenophobia
fear of getting into the wrong queue

This may sound like a mere foible, but, be assured, it is not. The **agmenophobe** will agonise for some minutes – even hours in extreme cases – before committing to one particular queue, for fear that it might be slower than the others. Some doctors think there is a little of the **agmenophobe** in all of us: to be fair, few people can honestly say that they have never found themselves trying to get money from a bank with numerous cashpoints and not, at some point, been temporarily convinced that they were going to get in the slow queue? Also, once in the queue, who can claim never to have anxiously eyed up the others in a bid to monitor q.d.r.?* Many long-term **agmenophobes** will always go to the cashpoint with a friend, who will act as their 'queue dummy' in another lane, to reduce their odds. There is a variant form of the disease, *agmenophobia specifica*, in which the sufferer not only has a fear of getting into or being in the slow queue, but actively thinks that it may be slower *because* they are in it. These people need your sympathy.

[orig. der.: *agmen*, herd or flock]

*q.d.r.: queue dispersal rate

aliacallophobia
fear of not being as clever as the
company one keeps

Despite recently unearthed Viennese research to
the contrary, **aliacallophobia** is incurable (Freud
famously stated that **aliacallophobes** 'simply need
to smoke bigger cigars'). Sufferers are easily
spotted: they twitch at the mention of the name
Ruth Lawrence. They consider dinner parties the
front line. An unfortunate seating plan can 'transport the aliacallophobe back to the school play-
ground'.* Psychiatrists suggest reading every
newspaper for a week, prior to any dinner appointment, but this can only do so much. Someone
only need mention 'the Middle East situation',
for example, and **aliacallophobes** know they are
sunk. Radical Cambridge professor Stephen
Indoles recommends learning one subject and
aggressively pushing it to the top of the agenda,
all night (*Playing Your Joker*, Cranium Press,
1969), but this strategy requires careful appli-
cation. Most **aliacallophobes** prefer to gen up on
interesting, trivial facts, to deflect attention from

*quote from Stephen Fry's *Boy – Girl – Boy – Genius*
(Polyglot Press, 1996)

virtually any unknown subject (known as the 'QI' method). Nevertheless, a careless comment (such as, 'Did you know Jeanette Krankie has an IQ of 192?') can easily scupper any good work.

[orig. der.: *alia*, another; *callere*, to know]

—◀◦▶—

alterdissemophobia
fear of missing something on another channel

This is a very modern phobia, made possible by the advent of ever more sophisticated remote controls. Previously, the nuclear family would 'flick' (change channels) once or twice a night at best, the bother and sheer physical effort of having to get up and walk over to the television set far outweighing the gains to be made. Nowadays, though, every break is the cue for a virtual strobe-fest of channel-hopping – or multi-flicking, as doctors call it. Many think it is as much a factor in the phenomenal rise of RSI in children as texting. It has also led to a blurring of the lines between television and life, with growing numbers of teachers reporting that when pupils leave classes to go to the toilet, they request that the teacher pauses the lesson. The Sky remote (available on some private health schemes) has made it slightly better for families of sufferers, as it means the **alterdissemophobe** can skate along through other channels at the bottom of the screen without changing the existing programme, in order to see what is on elsewhere. This has the effect of turning the sufferer from actual **alterdissemophobe** to mere annoying twat.

[orig. der.: *alter*, another; *disseminere*, to broadcast]

◄◦►

amipartophobia
fear of sharing friends

'To err is human, to forgive, divine'. To share . . . is worthy of fast-track beatification. **Ami-partophobia** goes something like this:

You introduce Ned, your life-and-soul-of-the-party friend, to X and Y, minor-league pals. Some time later, X and Y let slip that they're nursing hangovers after last night's dinner party 'with Ned'. Maybe they know another Ned, you briefly hope. The smile that draws across your face is not so much starched as 'had a minor stroke'. *Ned* Ned? 'Yes, isn't Ned fab?' they chime. The words brand themselves on your skin. Ned is *your* hangover buddy. Surely they understood that when you introduced them? At a stretch, he's joint ownership, available for events which you *and* the minor leaguers will be attending, surely? Now, if you fall out, who gets custody of Ned?

Welcome to the world of **amipartophobia**. Few cures exist. Some doctors recommend throwing a dinner party – inviting Ned plus minor leaguers – and then, while the Nigella is still tripping through the small intestine, engaging Ned in various Proustian reminiscences of legendary times between the two of you. ('Oh, Ned . . . remember *Filthy Phoebe!!!*') If this doesn't work, admit it: you never liked Ned anyway.

[orig. der.: *amicus*, friend; *partire*, to share]

—◦—

antefamaphobia
fear that people were talking about you but stopped just before you entered the room

An awfully long fear, but one which can render its victims speechless and uneasily shifting from foot to foot in moments. A surprising number of people suffer from this – and not just your average paranoiacs. Far from it. In fact, many can probably point to a time when, on entering a room full of people they knew, they had more than just a vague feeling that one or two of them had just shut up and were now nervously rearranging their hair, or whistling one of those non-tunes much favoured by taxi-drivers. **Antefamaphobia** is a sad disease, and it is not unknown for **antefamaphobes** to break down in tears while watching old Westerns, when they witness the pianist stop playing the moment the stranger enters the saloon. Amazingly, it is also suffered in reverse, in which instance it is called *antefamaphobia contrarius*. *Contrarius* sufferers fear that they will be talked about as soon as they leave the room. Interestingly enough, these are often the same people who cannot resist peering in through the crack of the fridge door, as it closes, to see if the light *is* going to go off.

[orig. der.: *ante*, before; *fama*, rumour]

‑‑◦‑‑

aperepiphobia
fear of opening email

Not dissimilar to **versurphobia** (q.v.), but much more wide-ranging. **Aperepiphobes** are people who fear any email, from mere spam to important stuff from the boss. They simply fear the unknown nature of the as yet unopened message. It's such a shame. Emails can be delightful: long-lost friends getting in touch, news from that sweet little baby goat you adopted, an offer of a penis extension (as one media executive recently said, It's annoying – so many emails offering penis extensions and yet only so many you can take up). Yet in our computer-dominated workplaces, where the person staring you in the face at the desk opposite will happily send you an electronic missive to say pass the paper clips, emails can also channel lots of crap: notice of things the boss says you have to do; notice of things the boss says you haven't done; notice of things the boss says if you don't do soon, you'll soon have nothing to do ever again. So, pity the **aperepiphobe** who hears that 'ping' telling them they have mail and feels a shiver run down their spine. Be kind to them. Maybe drop them an email.

[orig. der.: *aperire*, to open; *epistula*, letter]

◄○►

aquadormophobia
fear of dribbling whilst asleep on a train

As Latin scholars will see, this phobia gets its name from a coming-together of the words *dormio* (all to do with napping) and *aqua* (all to do with, in this instance, an embarrassing length of gob). The truly cruel aspect of aquadormophobia stems from the fact that it is not preventable. At the precise moment sufferers need their fear to kick in, they fall asleep. Before they know it, they've had a pleasant dream about eating ice creams in the sun, their shirt is moist and the person opposite is smiling uncomfortably. A 1987 World Health Organisation report highlighted a four-fold increase in this debilitating phobia, which is known chiefly to strike 45–54-year-old, overweight men, usually between 5.47 p.m. and 7.17 p.m., and mainly on the way home to Basingstoke. A less common but more virulent strain is *alter aquadormophobia*, in which the sufferer fears the moment they wake to find that they have inadvertently fallen asleep on the shoulder of a fellow passenger, and, subsequently, dribbled on *him*. Results of recent trials of 'Wake Me Up at My Stop' badges, available to some sleeping passengers in a recent pilot scheme pioneered by one forward-thinking rail company, have encouraged plans to issue, in the next wave, versions bearing the legends 'Please Rouse Me if I Snore' and even 'Please Strike Me if I Dribble'.

[orig. der.: *aqua*, water; *dormire*, to sleep; *alter*, the other]

<0>

arcaphobia
fear of using the cashpoint towards the end of the month

Arcaphobia most often develops during student years, when the cashpoint card is less a means to access money and more a trophy to bandy round as a symbol of adulthood. The mismanagement of funds, then, an integral part of the student oath, often results in the first signs of **arcaphobia**. If you carry the disease with you into later life, the symptoms can be cruel. Sufferers tend not to opt for cashpoints where there is a queue, and they certainly never use a cashpoint within a shop. If the **arcophobe** *does* have to about-face from the cashpoint with no money, they will often be heard swearing before mumbling something along the lines of '. . . just . . . checking my balance'. Ultimately, the only cure is to keep tabs on one's money – which, for an **arcophobe**, is akin to asking them to keep count of how many breaths they take each month, and not to go over ten thousand: it's never going to happen. Amazingly, millionaire racehorse owner the Aga Sahga is still said to be a bit of an **arcophobe**, hence the names of some of his horses (Insufficient Funds, for example, and triple Derby winner, Refer to Bank). **Arcophobes** tend to hibernate in January.

[orig. der.: *arca*, strongbox or coffers]

bulliphobia
fear of not having the remote control

Despite the term translating as a fear of buttons, it is an absence of buttons that the **bulliphobic** male dreads (the full name, in fact, is *bulliphobia* *absens*). Entirely a male disease, a **bulliphobe's** symptoms include: Dead Man's Hand, where a sufferer's hand involuntarily starts to flap or twitch for the remote at the first sign of an advert; endless flicking (channel-hopping); and, of course, taking the remote with them into the kitchen. **Bulliphobia,** isolated by doctors at the Sony University for Teledisorders, Osaka during the early eighties, splits into two strains: *simplex* and *alter*. The latter, *b.a.*, is the most common, stemming from the male's desire for his remote being thwarted by child displacement or deep-cushioned sofas (some sufferers hanker for early, prototype videos, where remotes were connected via leads to the base unit). *B.s.* is less common and occurs when the male is forced to devolve use of the remote to a cohabiting partner. Doctors warn against encouraging this syndrome as it leads to the more pronounced *bulliphobia simplex extra*, which in turn manifests itself in high anxiety levels, tantrums and, if the partner continues, heavy snoring.

[orig. der.: *bullae*, buttons]

—◀○▶—

cadophobia
fear of failure

Driven people are *not* **cadophobes**. They are simply driven people. **Cadophobes**, most often, do not drive themselves. They fear failure so much that they have convinced themselves they should not even try. They can't fail at something if they haven't even had a go, right? As a result, they are often to be found in bars, regaling people with details of how they 'had an idea once that would have revolutionised the graphics industry' or what have you, only they 'never got round to it'. Of course they didn't. **Cadophobes** usually end up becoming

the most cynical of cynics, the Waldorf and Stadlers
of their circle, always on hand to tell people how
badly they are doing. As the saying goes, the road
to hell is lined with **cadophobes** telling you they
could have shown you a better route.

[orig. der.: *cadere*, to fail]

◄○►

caerulophobia
fear of Tories

This is up there with **euaxophobia** (q.v.) in that
caerulophobes do not actively seek a cure.
Although, medically speaking, this is not a friendly
fear, to the **caerulophobe** it is. In much the same
way that the creators of *Spitting Image* felt able
to write a song in the eighties called 'I've Never
Met a Nice South African', so thinks the **caerulophobe** about Conservatives. Seated next to a
stranger at a wedding, for example, they can often
get on like a house on fire, until the point at which
a tell-tale comment lets slip that person's political
allegiance (it might be something harmless like how
statistics show that lethal injection can work as a
viable deterrent to the crime of dropping litter).
At this point, the **caerulophobe** reinterprets their

entire series of dealings with the subject, very often changing the subject with a line like, 'Did you know the meaning of the word Tory is outlaw?' Very much a North/South divide disease, and often seen in conjunction with **contumaphobia** (q.v.).

[orig. der.: *caerulius*, blue]

◄●►

calvophobia
fear of going bald

Not surprisingly, this is almost entirely a male fear. If you want to find a **calvophobe**, go to a mirror: he's usually there, combing (gently) to check the current state of play, as it were. Many **calvophobes** will already have spent years visiting the barber, saying the words 'oh, just a trim, please' before they finally admit they have the disease. Often they ask to take home the shorn locks – reportedly as a memento, but in fact they are hoping to have them cryogenically frozen in case trichology is ever available on the NHS. The next stage is 'wash and don't go', during which the sufferer spends an inordinately long time staring at the hairs that have come out following a hair wash, like Keats looking tragically at a

Grecian urn. At this point, **calvophobes** take one of two routes: they either follow the god of comb-over, St Bobby of Charlton, and stock up on Elton John CDs, or they decide to go *inverse commando* and wear nothing on top. In the seventies, great work was done in this latter field by pioneering slapheads Yul Brynner and Telly Savalas, although their groundbreaking achievements were nearly ruined with the arrival of Duncan Goodhew.

[orig. der.: *calvus*, bald]

canusophobia
fear of going grey

It used to be accepted wisdom that **canusophobia** struck, as the saying went, 'when the first white sheep enters the fold'. Nowadays, though, doctors report that it is more often diagnosed when the patient has just met an old friend who has gone grey. The sight of a pal from university who was frequently mistaken for a flock of ravens but who now resembles a negative of himself can be enough to trigger **canusophobia**. Symptoms include longer periods spent in front of the bathroom mirror. Added to this, **canusophobes** are often afflicted with a timidity bordering on the medical which sees them unable to decide whether to pull or not to pull – a grey hair out, that is. They fear that if they do, three more will spring up in its place, a medical phenomena known as 'anus syndrome' (not what it might seem: see below). One of the saddest symptoms of **canusophobia** in women is what doctors call the *alluo* effect, the cruel way in which the brain tricks the female sufferer into thinking her newly greyed hair might somehow look better were it to be given a bizarre, electric-blue rinse.

[orig. der.: *canus*, grey; *anus*, old wife; *alluo*, rinse]

carpenasophobia
fear that people can see you
picking your nose

This is now totally eradicated amongst motorists.

[orig. der.: *carpe nasum*, seize the nose]

ceterinfanophobia
fear of other people's children

This occasional fear strikes all areas of society:
single, married, childless, blessed, etc. It should
also be said that one cannot suffer **ceterinfanophobia** over one's own children: they are

flawless and not to be feared. They can be feared by someone else, obviously, at which point they cease to attract plaudits and start attracting asbos. This is the central dual nature of **ceterinfanophobia**: other people's children are rude, yours are merely 'spirited'; other people's children attempt grievous bodily harm, yours 'like a little rough and tumble'. And so on. Sufferers can often be recognised by their starched smile, worn as armour against a staring seven-year-old who has just said something painfully honest about them. While they were trying to read the Sunday papers. In peace. Most **ceterinfanophobes** grit their teeth and recite the mantra: 'I love children, I just can't eat a whole one. I love children, I just . . .'

[orig. der.: *ceteri*, others; *infans*, child]

civerophobia
fear of not being politically correct

Thought to have originated at the BBC, **civero-phobia** has the habit of creeping up on its victims. *Civerophobia prudens* is one of the Partridge family of phobias, so called because they are best illustrated by the television character Alan Partridge. *Prudens* sufferers are overly aware of non-PC phraseology and consequently are easily spotted by their conversation. They duck and dive between faltering explanations, forever verbally ambushing themselves, trying to explain what they *weren't* meaning whilst at the same time highlighting their fear to those who wouldn't otherwise have thought anything of it. *Civerophobia octogenaria* is a related, proxy fear which most often strikes the next of kin of the elderly, who fear that their relatives will, at any moment, come out with a spectacularly non-PC opinion, possibly in the presence of a clergyman. *Civerophobia octogenaria propinqua* is the knock-on, rare but disabling fear that they, the sufferer, *share* the same non-PC opinion as their relatives, for illogical genetic reasons. This disease often manifests itself in recurring nightmares in which the patient is caught in a busy public place dressed as Eddie

Booth from the seventies television series *Love Thy Neighbour*.

[orig. der.: *civilis*, political; *verum*, true]

◄◦►

civiliphobia
fear of politicians

Another of the friendly fears, this phobia has increased exponentially since the late sixties. It's often jokingly said that, in any random survey of three people, two will be **civiliphobes** and the third a politician. Symptoms include increased levels of scepticism, an aversion to Sunday lunchtime television and, often, the desire to holiday during a general election. Some chronic cases have been known to twitch in the presence of rosettes. In the nineties, two new strains were identified at Angel University (formerly Islington Tech): *civiliphobia nova labor*, in which not only politicians but also their entire entourage and backroom staff were feared; and *civiliphobia verso*, which can send sufferers into a spinning fit. One common symptom of the former appears to be a propensity to march (often in Hyde Park). The only known beneficial side effect of *civiliphobia nova labor* was thought to be the potential emigration of Paul Daniels et al., although this has not been proven/realised. (See also **maginvalophobia,** q.v.)

[orig. der.: *civilis*, political; *versare*, to spin]

◄○►

coetusermophobia
fear of call centres

This is not **inanophobia** (q.v.), nor Davey's **depoconchophobia** (q.v.). This is, purely and simply, fear of the whole call-centre culture and what it can do to you. **Coetusermophobes** dread call-centre operatives' refusal to inhabit the world of free will. Some fear the inability to talk to real people. Some fear the 'ring cycle', the endless spiral of despair entered when they have stayed on hold so long they are cut off, thus requiring them to call again, and so on. (Any similarity to a series of Wagner operas of the same name is not coincidental.) The vast majority of sufferers fear one thing above all others: hearing the words 'I'm sorry, I'm not autho-rised to do that' (I.S.I.N.A.T.D.T.). These words can trigger a **coetusermophobic fit.** Someone expe-riencing such a fit will typically be frothing at the mouth, banging the receiver on the desk, demanding to be put through to a manager (I.S.I.N.A.T.D.T.) and experiencing early onset senile dementia. Incidentally, the 'ring cycle' is not to be confused with the 'tone poem.' The 'tone poem' is an occasional phenomenon whereby a patient can inadvertently become caught in a predetermined formula of robotically intoned messages leading back to the very first message the sufferer heard when they first started to hold, often several days ago. The messages form a type of trance-inducing poem (hence the name). It is an unfortunate process, thought to have been developed by the CIA in the early seventies as a form of brainwashing technique.

[orig. der.: *coetus*, meeting; *sermo*, speech]

-◄◦►-

colligaphobia
fear of packing

There is no point trying to identify this as either a male or female disease since, to be fair, only men pack. Women do not pack. They repack. Regardless, **colligaphobia** affects mainly 35–44-year-old, ABC1 married males. They seem to be afflicted with the notion that a suitcase is simply a suitcase, whereas the 35–44 ABC1 female knows it is more than this: it is a mystic puzzle and only they have had the solution revealed to them in a dream. As a result, the 35–44-year-old ABC1 male eventually becomes **colligaphobic,** fearful even of suggesting what the case's contents might be in case they are mistaken. This transcription, of a *trigger* conversation, was secretly recorded by the Valise Institute, the right-wing think tank for packing:

F: 'How many pairs of trousers do you want?'

M: 'Three?'

F: 'Three? Why three?'

M: 'Well . . . two then?'

F: 'Two?'

M: 'What then?'

F: 'You'll need four, plus your suit and some shorts. Now, shirts. How many shirts? Ben? . . . Ben? . . . What are you doing with that noose?'

You can fight **colligaphobia,** but it is best not to. Many have tried taking up Tetris or watching old copies of *The Krypton Factor* in the hope of discovering some sort of secret in the puzzle round. There have been known instances where men have recovered, but all too often they are set back years when a customs official innocently asks whether they packed their bag them-selves. Better to find your local branch of CASE (Colligaphobics Against Suitcase Equality, motto: 'Pack it In'), where you will be encouraged to 'leave out the clothes you want packed' then taken through the Six Steps. (Step One, your doorstep. Step Two, the pub doorstep, and so on.)

[org. der.: *colligare*, to collect or assemble]

-◄○►-

congressiophobia
fear of meetings

Despite the seemingly endless number of levels and hierarchies in the contemporary workplace – VP, CEO, Account Executive, etc. – most modern businesses are actually filled with people who operate on one of only two levels. Firstly, there are those whose job it is to set up and attend meet-ings. This activity constitutes around 90 per cent of their workload, so once you add in drinking coffee, surfing the Internet and, of course, debriefing after meetings, that is more or less their full-time job. Then, secondly, there are those whose job it is to attend these same meetings, but who must also do all the work that arises from them. These people are generally **congressiophobes**. They fear not just attendance at but the very existence of meetings. They are often recognised by a) their brusque tone, b) their playing of 'Wankword Bingo' – they will be the ones shouting 'House!' when someone mentions 'low-hanging fruit' – or c) their absence. A recent offshoot, *congressiophobia cerebratempa* (*c.c.*), is the fear of brainstorming sessions. Sufferers have been known to break down at the mere utterance of the phrase, 'There's no such thing as a bad idea.' Indeed, police think the recent death of the boss of a small IT company in Cardiff, Cursor Major Plc, may have had something to do with him having recently overcome his *c.c.*. His last words were apparently, 'There's no "I" in team,' whereupon he was beaten to death with a flip chart.

[orig. der.: *congressio*, meeting; *cerebrum*, brain; *tempestas*, storm]

–◦–

conspecunophobia
fear of putting money in the collection

It is cunningly cruel. The part of a church service where you hand over the cash is immediately preceded by the warmest, fuzziest section of the whole shebang: the smiley handshaking. (Some folk even up sticks and try for the odd snog). Your clammy-handed neighbour, however, may not be enjoying one second of this temporary love-fest. All they can think of is . . . the collection. **Conspecunophobes** are not necessarily stingy (though many obviously are), but they may *fear* being stingy, of just being *seen* as stingy. Symptoms of **conspecunophobia** include nervous coughing, disarmingly flamboyant hand flourishes (distraction technique) and, rarely, pointing out a cute, small child with the free hand, in order to divert attention. **Conspecunophobes** can get through a purse-type collection relatively painlessly, but open baskets – favoured by particularly sadistic collectors – can provoke panic attacks and cries of, 'Look, the Queen only gives a fiver!!' Chronic **conspecunophobes** load their children with motley collections of loose change, to give the impression that they are donating their life savings; chances are they are not. *Conspecunophobia officina* is a separate strain, common during workplace collections for departing colleagues. Use of A4 envelopes for collecting has made spotting it all but impossible.

[orig. der.: *conscius*, conscious or knowing; *pecunia*, money; *officina*, workshop]

contumaphobia
fear of agreeing with right-wing columnists

Contumaphobia is what is known as an occasional fear, suffered chiefly by those who don't buy right-wing papers themselves but know people who do. As a result, they come across them only from time to time, and the affliction occurs in small but violent pockets. Just one frothing piece – on asylum seekers, falling house prices on the ocean bed or the ban on calling Christmas Island by its name for fear of religious offence – and a **contumaphobic** attack can occur. **Contumaphobia** is, of course, much more prevalent amongst those who come into contact with the 'blue press' more regularly – i.e. famous people, members of the media, homeless people who have switched to them for their insulation since the *Guardian* went Berliner. Radio 4, previously thought to be a haven for **contumaphobes**, recently found evidence to the contrary when it conducted an on-air poll to find the best usage for the Millenium Dome site. This resulted in the majority of callers opting against a concert venue in favour of a fully functioning recreation of the Tyburn gallows.

[orig. der.: *conciere*, to move or stir up; *tumultuosus*, commotion or uproar]

crunumuliphobia
fear that every time you turn on the telly you'll see Carol Vorderman

Thankfully, this is not as common as it used to be in the nineties, when there was a virtual epidemic. The term for this malaise was actually inspired by the Icelandic practice of forming new words. There, a state-appointed committee meets to ensure the purity of the native language. (The country, possibly quite wisely, insists on refusing new, foreign words, preferring to decide locally on what the Icelandic word for, say, computer will be.) The BMA took this as a model when they met to decide on the word for this new and worrying phobia, but looked to Latin for their inspiration. As a result, it is a conglomeration of three words: *cruentus*, bloody; *numeri*, numbers; and *mulier*, woman – altogether, then, fear of seeing that bloody numbers woman. Although very much on the wane now, many an old, male sufferer will still get a twinge around four in the afternoon. In places, it has been supplanted by **formicorniphobia** (q.v.).

[orig. der.: *cruentus*, bloody; *numeri*, numbers; *mulier*, woman]

deditophobia
fear of becoming hooked on something

Nothing major, you understand. This fear is of becoming hooked on something trivial or trashy. Something you know you shouldn't even be thinking of. *Hello!* magazine, for example. Or *'I'm a Celebrity, Get Me out of Here'*. Or Pot Noodle. A **deditophobe** will promise themselves they wont watch: 'Not this time,' they say when it comes to the latest series of *The X Factor*. They may safely navigate Saturday evening to miss the programme, and even effortlessly avoid the results part later on. Then they arrive at work on Monday morning and the entire, brainless office is talking about it. 'Nonsensenonsense . . . Sharon Osbourne . . . inanebollocks . . . Oh, that Shane is amazzzzin' . . . bollockstoshtwaddle . . . Don't those girls look like blokes!! . . . Baloneygarbageclaptrapkak . . .' Well, it's hard, isn't it? Not to become hooked, I mean. Isn't it? *No, it's not!* It's easy. I'd rather pierce my earlobes with a hole punch. Get a grip.

[orig. der.: *deditus*, devoted]

‹◦›

depoconchophobia
fear of putting a phone down

Thanks to answerphones, **depoconchophobia** is rare. This pitiless terror chains victims to a receiver more effectively than even a computer helpline. **Depoconchophobes** fear that the person they are calling may answer *at any time*, despite the fact that the phone has been ringing endlessly. So they are afraid to put the phone down. Many hear ghost answers, convinced that someone picked up just as they replaced the receiver. They instantly put it back to their ear, with a hopeful 'Hello?' A specific type is **Davey's depoconchophobia**: fear of putting down the phone *while on hold* (named after the person who first isolated the strain, when kept on hold to Directory Enquiries for over three hours in 1972). Some D.d. sufferers have night-mares in which Alexander Graham Bell anounces that, although Mr Watson cannot come to the phone right now, your call is important to them. Chronic cases will not put seashells to their ear for fear that the sea will put them in a queue, to be answered shortly. *Depoconchophobia contraria* is a related fear, common amongst mobile users, of not having pressed the button to end the call. Sufferers will often endure several minutes of silence, shushing all in sight, before they are satisfied that it is safe to carry on talking. Non-sufferers have been known inadvertently to tell important work colleagues exactly what they think of them without realising they were being overheard.

NOTE: it is, ironically, from **depoconchophobia** that doctors first coined the term 'hang-up'.

[orig. der.: *deponere*, to put down; *concha*, shell]

◄◦►

deversoraphobia
fear of hotels

A 2004 IHMA (International Hotel/Motel Association) study, 'Room for Improvement', showed that instances of **deversoraphobia** have increased by 40 per cent in the last ten years and predicts that, if the trend continues, entire hotel chains will be forced out of business. **Deversoraphobia** still tends to be known as the 'businessman's phobia', with over 80 per cent of sufferers being long-term corporate travellers. Most can no longer watch CNN without feeling an irrational need to cry, and some say it has even ruined their delight in having the remote control at home (see **bulliphobia**, q.v.). Many say a minibar is no longer a thing of beauty, and some have even trodden the path to rock-star room-trashing – the corporate version, of course – by cynically and deliberately unplugging their Corby trouser presses. Chronic **deversoraphobes** cannot listen to the lyrics of 'Hotel California' without exhibiting violent behaviour, and others go to the extent of paying complete strangers to dine with them, simply out of fear of hearing the words 'Table for one?' from the restaurant's maitre d'. *Deversoraphobia barbapictura*, though it partly shares the name, is in fact unconnected. *D.v.* sufferers fear a dodgy movie appearing on a bill for which they will have to claim expenses. Symptoms include a tendency only to watch the hotel television for four minutes at a time and belief that the phrase *Debbie Does Dallas* is in fact spelt 'sundries'.

[orig. der.: *deversorium*, inn; *barbarus*, rude; *pictura*, picture]

◄○►

discimedicophobia
fear of student doctors

Not fear of doctors (common and perfectly under-standable), nor fear of students (rare but potent), but fear of what the two, combined, might do to you. **Discimedicophobes** view a student doctor and see someone who must have been eating chips in curry sauce with his scalpel while washing down barrels of Guinness in the university bar – just before coming on to the ward. They would no more allow themselves to be inspected by a student doctor than they would fly with a student pilot. Most cannot even cope with student doctors in the room as observers, preferring to interpret it as mere perverted voyeurism. Symptoms include *hearing reinterpretation*, whereby a patient's ears translate a doctor's words before they reach the brain. For example, to many **discimedicophobes**, the phrase 'Do you mind if my student doctor sits in?' might as well comes across as 'Can I film you naked for national television?'

[orig. der.: *medicus*, doctor; *discipulus*, student]

◄○►

discipulophobia
fear of students

Discipulophobia is prevalent in all echelons of society except amongst 18–21-year-old, ABC1 males and females. Otherwise, it is more or less universal, although some say modern-day **discip-ulophobes** have a harder time of it, as students are so much harder to spot. The days of the ill-fitting, charity overcoat-wearing, bespectacled, *Socialist Worker*-selling scamp of dubious hygiene, trying to pay for a National Express return to Newcastle with a whisky bottle full of small change, have gone. Now the object of fear is more likely to resemble the classic eighties yuppy in all but floppy-fringed quiff, complete with iPod, mobile and BlackBerry, although they still try to pay for a National Express return to Newcastle with a whisky bottle of small change.

[orig. der.: *discipulus*, student]

--o--

diveruphobia
fear of admitting the truth

On a very mundane level, we have all refused to admit we were wrong at some point, backing ourselves into an argument cul-de-sac and refusing to take the only route out. This is not **diveruphobia**. This is just bloody-mindedness. True **diveruphobia** manifests itself in wholly more harmful ways. A middle-aged man, for example, desperate to appear youthful by wearing inappropriate clothing labels and attempting to use street language – even though he works in insurance – is, as well as being a potential **senecophobe** (q.v.), most definitely a **diveruphobe**. Government ministers can become **diveruphobic**, often just before leaving office. Once they hear the PM issuing his 'full and unqualified support' in a public statement, the phobia tends to kick in. The minister fights on and on, in a desperate attempt to deny, or sometimes redefine, the truth of a certain matter, occasionally using their children or family as props. Thankfully, their **diveruphobia** is usually temporary.

[orig. der.: *dicere*, to tell; *verum*, truth]

◂◦▸

donoculophobia
fear of eye contact

Only a small proportion of society experiences **donoculophobia** in its purest sense – a simple, unexplained fear of eye contact that will see a sufferer staring at the ceiling as they talk to some-body or, alternatively, constantly scanning the floor as if they have lost a contact lens. More often than not, though, a **donoculophobe** is afflicted with one of the lesser forms of the disease. *Donoculophobia foetia* sufferers fear eye contact because of the vile stench they have just created; *donoculophobia malnuntia* patients struggle because they are bearers of bad news (many bosses develop *d.m.* at times of lay-offs), and *schola donoculophobes* fear eye contact with a teacher. In this last instance, eye contact reminds the teacher of their existence and, subsequently, their availability for answering the next question. Nothing to do with **ocuviaphobia** (q.v.).

[orig. der.: *donare*, to give; *oculus*, eye; *schola*, school; *foetere*, to stink; *male*, bad; *mintius*, news]

41

duxophobia
fear of your boss

No matter how well you get on with your boss or pride yourself on your special relationship, you can never actually be friends. There is always the possibility that the boss might get out of the wrong side of bed one day and think, 'Mmm, this Weetabix is a little on the chewy side . . . I think I'll sack what's-his-face.' Any number of factors can influence a boss's opinion of you: the car you drive, the argument they had with their partner, the way you said 'good morning' when you got in the lift. As a result, most working relationships run on **duxophobia**. In moderation, it is manageable; indeed, some would say it is healthy. In excess, however, it can lead to all manner of problems, and you become like a Cabinet Minister in the Thatcher government.

[orig. der.: *dux*, chief]

-‹o›-

euaxophobia
fear of posh people

Often mistaken for fear of wealth, **euaxophobia** takes its name from the Latin cry 'Euax!', or 'Hurrah!' It is said that, in ancient Rome, the rather well-to-do Euan made himself unpopular with both his blasé attitude to wealth and his roseate cheeks. (When the plebs could abide 'Euax' Euan no longer, he was sentenced to a weekly cheek-slapping.) Nowadays, it is very much a North-South divide affair, and the epicentre of **euaxophobia** is thought to be Gateshead. **Euaxophobia** is nasty because it attacks all the senses: patients become touchy when they hear an RP accent, they get a strange taste in their mouths when they drink Pimm's, they see red over a mud-spattered 4x4 in the city and they become positively nauseous at the smell of a Barbour.

[orig. der.: *euax*, hurrah]

◄○►

excirculophobia
fear of not being picked

A very common fear that starts in school but can, in some cases, stay with people to the grave. It is based on the fear that, yes, you are clearly crap, and not only will you not be picked, but you do not even deserve to be. Most of us have been there – we all have those pockets in our memory, often triggered by seeing an old school pal in the street. They pop up in your head and bark, 'Hey, look. It's Joseph Catterill. He was FAR better at football than you. You were always in the last two, unpicked and unloved. It was either you or the kid with asthma who could only run for thirteen seconds before lying down. AND . . . they chose him first. AND . . . the other team gave you away with him, as a job lot.' Gosh, it can stay with you, can't it? Amazingly, it stays on well into many sufferers' working lives, too. Some say it was behind Ellen MacArthur's decision, when deciding on her options for games day at school, to choose transatlantic rowing over hockey. ('MacArthur . . . *MacArthur* . . . Anyone seen MacArthur?' 'She's just off the Cape of Good Hope, sir.' 'Absent.') In corporate Britain, it is said that many tree-hugging, staff-training specialists are reformed **excirculophobes**, desperately shouting 'Go at the speed of the slowest' and 'There's no "I" in team' to a group of lifeless, shabby-suited sloths who only signed up for a free night in a cheap hotel.

[orig. der.: *circulus*, group]

—◦—

exercitophobia
fear of exercise

Not to be confused with either laziness or 'being a fat bastard', **exercitophobia** has its roots in the belief that exercise is an ancient art and something best left to the experts. **Exercitophobes** are often most easily identified at work, as they tend to have humorous signs above their desks, saying things like 'I love work – I can watch it for hours'. Interestingly, one of the common side-effects of **exercitophobia** is a complete expert knowledge of how one particular sport should be played, financed, managed and run, from the ground upwards – particularly football. Strangely, this particular side-effect usually goes hand in hand with a medical condition which prevents the sufferer from actually participating in the sport.

[orig. der.: *exercitatio*, exercise]

—◦—

exiturrophobia
fear that one's willy is too small

Every man on the planet has, at some time or other, suffered from **exiturrophobia**. Anyone who says they haven't is either a **diveruphobe** (q.v.) or perhaps John Holmes. As its definition suggests, this is exclusively a male disorder for which there is only one known cure: sex. This does the trick for most **exiturrophobes**, proving that their *instrumenta nuptiae* is not only in good working order but, in fact, doesn't do too bad a job either. Sadly, a small minority find that they are suffering from **graphicoitophobia** (q.v.); these tend to be mainly estate agents and traffic wardens.

[orig. der.: *exilis*, small or meagre; *turris*, tower]

—◆—

expellophobia
fear of going to the loo in someone else's house

The number of people who have seen a lovely evening out ruined by **expellophobia** is legion – so many, indeed, that it is hard not to consider many stories to be mere urban myths.

Expellophobes could tell you that this is not the case (as could **abcellophobes**, q.v.). If they ever dare to use a *foreign* loo (any other than their own), they will first have studied the form for some time beforehand. Some will have watched the guests' toilet pattern – mentally noting length of time spent *en toilette*, intervals, etc. – for more than half the evening before being prepared to make their move. Once committed, they will often stay *in camera* for an age before daring to re-appear. Die-hard sufferers simply never use the loo *abroad*, so to speak, preferring to grin and bear it, and attempting to pass off their troll-like, rumbling stomach with comments about the neighbours moving furniture around. Any self-respecting **expellophobe** will always refuse to go to the loo if visiting a bungalow.

[orig. der.: *expellere*, to expel]

-◄o►-

exterviaphobia
fear of leaving the middle lane

Exterviaphobia is a tricky little thing. It is one of the few phobias which does not cause the sufferer to believe they are ill. As a result, it is seldom diagnosed and never cured. In the small number of instances where an **exterviaphobe** has any realisation that they have the disease, therapists often refuse to take on the patient. They simply say it is up to us, the vast majority of healthy motorists, to drive our vehicles 'up the arse' of the **exterviaphobe's** car and flash our headlights at them. In extreme cases, they will even recommend overtaking them, cutting in front of them and sweeping over to the inside lane, just to make the point. It will do little to help, though. An **exterviaphobe** is like Linus, and the middle lane is their blanket. Yes, they will venture out of it when going round bends (they find it easier to steer right while in the outside lane, or left while in the inside lane) or when in heavy traffic. Other than that, they see no reason to leave their favoured 'heart of the road'. Interestingly, you can often spot an **exterviaphobe** even when on foot. For example, when you enter a department store, there are often three doors by which to enter. If someone has left the middle door locked (why do they do that?), the **exterviaphobe** will often be the one stood outside, scratching his head and trying to figure out how to get in.

[orig. der.: *exterior*, outside; *via*, street]

◄○►

exuerphobia
fear of undressing

For most doctors, this is the easiest phobia to diagnose, not least because the patients refuse to let themselves be examined. This fear would be easily understood, too, were it not for the fact that many sufferers who profess that they are unable to peel off their clothes when the lights are way down low, as it were, are the very same people who then proceed to walk around the house naked. Doctors can do little for the average **exuerphobe** save recommending that they try turning up the central heating. Not to be confused with **nuduphobia** (q.v.).

[orig. der.: *exuere*, to strip]

—<o>—

fabaphobia
fear of ordering in coffee shops

This translates as 'fear of the bean', due largely to the ancient Romans having no word for coffee. Fabaphobes are naive, old-fashioned types who feel they should be able to enter coffee shops – which they insist on calling cafés – and conjure up a beverage with the words 'Coffee, please'. How quaint. They are paralysed with fear when confronted by a *barista* (thankfully, most **fabaphobes** are unaware of what the person behind the bar is called; never enlighten them) using language like 'Venti? With wings?'* **Fabaphobes** need our help. Doctors advise that if you find yourself in the vicinity of someone you suspect is having a **fabaphobic** attack – they might be clinging on to the milk and napkin counter, glazing over at the nutmeg sprinkler or even frantically trying to find the word 'mochafreezer' in a dictionary – you should not try to move them. Suggest a 'nice cup of tea', then inform a member of the over-fifties.

* Trans: 'Large? To take away?'

[orig. der.: *faba*, bean]

◄○►

facipsophobia
fear of DIY

A **facipsophobe** can no more understand how one can possibly make a shelf stay up on a wall than how a jumbo jet might stay in the air. This failure to comprehend the basic laws of DIY prevents them from ever getting started on household projects. The ancient book *The Seven Periods of Sitting Down and Not Doing Much of Hercules* (the lost precursor to the *Seven Labours*) is thought to record the first known case of **facipsophobia**, ever. A genuine **facipsophobe** is not even sure that he can make a Rawlplug stay in a wall, let alone satisfy his wife's fantasies of 'knocking through.' In attempting a cure, therapists tend to get genuine facipsophobes started off on flatpacks, although not Ikea products (Ikea's rule of 'there should always be one crucial item missing' can set a sufferer back years). Remember, **facipsophobes** are genuine people, and not to be confused with those who simply feign the disease in order to get out of tiling a bathroom, etc. Therapists have a term for these people: *nothus ignavus*, (lit. work-shy bastards).

[orig. der.: *facere*, to make; *ipse*, self]

━◄○►━

falsuphobia
fear of being wrong

Largely suffered by women, the male form of this disease is thought to have died out as early as man's time in the Garden of Eden, when God basically pinned it all on Eve. As a result, women can and do occasionally suffer from a healthy fear of being wrong. Men, on the other hand, are different. If men do ever become **falsuphobes**, they find the compulsion to hide their illness overwhelming. For male politicians, particularly, the onset of **falsuphobia** usually coincides with a desire to spend more time with their family. Even rarer than the political **falsuphobe** is the taxi-driving falsuphobe – read *The Only Language They Understand* by Colin Stringer (Bigot Press, 1971) for more on the subject. On a historical note, it has often been pointed out that two of the greatest stateswomen in history had differing attitudes to falsuphobia: Queen Victoria and Margaret Thatcher. Psychologists now believe that Victoria's refusal to believe in the existence of lesbians was possibly a related form of the disease. Equally, the same psychologists believe Margaret Thatcher was incapable of understanding that there existed people who might ever fear being wrong, let alone simply that she herself might be mistaken.

[orig. der.: *falsus*, mistaken]

◄◊►

feruterphobia
fear of walking on the ground in bare feet

In the old days, this was often referred to as 'Toughguy's Toes', as it had the power to reduce even the hardest hardman to a pigeon dancing on a hot tin roof. This remains, still, one of the distinctive facets of **feruterphobia**. Its sufferers are all too aware that, compared to the Spanish Inquisition or being crushed under a wheel, walking on the ground in bare feet is not particularly onerous. Yet they cannot help it, especially on gravel surfaces – they 'ooh' and 'aah' their way across, arms outstretched, almost dancing, with the odd rich expletive peppering the air. **Feruterphobes** tend to be amazed that others *can* walk barefoot without the aid of a safety flip-flop. For them, it is a pitiless disease which frequently strikes when they are at their most vulnerable – in trunks or bikini. *Feruterphobia glarea* is a common summer strain in which sufferers are unable to cross a particular shingle section of an otherwise sandy beach. Thankfully, this rarely requires treatment as the effects are temporary, save for the loss of the odd 99. Also common is *feruterphobia calida*, in which the patient is unable to walk barefoot due to the heat of the sun-baked surface. All forms of

feruterphobia appear to attack men and children much more than women.

[orig. der.: *ferus*, ferocious; *terra*, ground; *glarea*, shingle; *calidus*, hot]

◄○►

finchartaphobia
fear of the loo paper running out

Some doctors refuse to admit that **finchartaphobia** exists, as they say it is a hunch at best and nobody actually *fears* running out of loo paper. Wrong. Think about it: you're in enemy territory (someone else's house) and you've done a huge one (very brave, see **expellophobia**, q.v.). You then realise there is only a certain amount of toilet paper left. So you start to fold, rather than scrunch up. You ration, strictly – two pieces per go and careful with it. If it gets worse, you split the two plys of the paper apart and then ration that. If you are unlucky enough to get 'reinforcements' (which is what self-help groups call a second tranche coming from the rear), then you will be glad you learnt how to carefully split apart and use the loo roll's cardboard holder during a childhood episode of *Blue Peter*. **Finchartophobia**, see? Doesn't exist? My arse.

[orig. der.: *finire*, to end; *chartae*, sheets of paper]

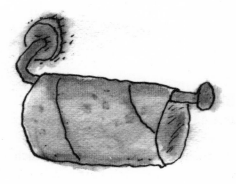

fistulaphobia
fear of the Underground

Do not for one minute confuse this with a fear of confined spaces. The **fistulaphobe** fears the smells, the people, the 'mind the gap' voice, the swaying of the handles hanging from the roof, the drivers' announcements, the fact that they don't even have time to board the train before a recorded announcement tells them to beware because the doors are closing. In short, they fear everything about the Tube. **Fistulaphobes** are, as a result, most often to be found in cars or on buses. Only when forced to use the Underground do they display symptoms: excessive journey-planning, nervous talking between stops, etc. Some sufferers will do anything to take their mind off their journey: a common trait of the **fistulaphobe** is that they know too much about the Tube map, such as obscure stations and station names backwards, for example. (It was a fistulaphobe who once told me that she was alighting at Krapy Rub Snif. I was slightly stunned until I realised it was Finsbury Park spelt backwards.) On the positive side, **fistulaphobes** do make excellent players of Mornington Crescent.

[orig. der.: *fistula*, tube]

forlatriphobia
fear of public toilets

Why there are some people left in the world who are *not* **forlatriphobes,** I do not know. Public loos are such tiny, dank and strange places, it is easy to see not only that **forlatriphobia** is on the increase but also how, in London, such places are constantly being turned into flats. The **forlatriphobe** fears any one of a number of things. Hygiene – which varies from pungently disinfected to 'are we above a recent burial site for plague victims?' – is obviously an issue. Potential lack of facilities is often cited, too, as is the whole 'loo-ser' issue (a loo-ser is a member of that peripheral underbelly of folk who seem to be almost resident in a public loo – they're there when you go in, they're still there when you leave). These days, most **forlatriphobes** admit they prefer to run a pub gauntlet, i.e., refusing to use a public convenience (often known as 'scrooging' because you never actually pay for anything). 'Scroogers' walk right through a pub, pretending to be customers but going straight to the toilets and back out again, even making as if to sit down to add authenticity.

[orig. der.: *foris*, in public; *latrina*, lavatory]

formicorniphobia

Modern-day version of **crunumuliphobia** (q.v.),
from Latin *formica* (meaning ant) and *omere* (deck).

—◦—

fortavocophobia
fear of speaking loudly while wearing
headphones

A very common phobia, particularly prevalent
among two groups: 45–54-year-old ABC1 joggers,
and *Kerrang*! readers. Anecdotal evidence also
suggests that at the average clay-pigeon shoot,
seven out of ten participants will be **fortavocophobes**. Sufferers realise they have the phobia in
various ways. Occasionally, they might find they
are constantly being 'shushed'. More often, they
whisper hello to a passer-by, only to see them
jump out of their skin. Side-effects include over-
compensating, whereby the sufferer will talk inordinately softly. People unaware that they are
singing, usually discordantly, while wearing headphones are often said to be suffering from a related
condition, *fortavocophobia ludibrium*, but this is
unproven. Younger generations, of course, are
unlikely to be **fortavocophobes**, having got used

to wearing headphones from the age of eighteen months.

[orig. der.: *fortis*, strong; *vocalis*, speaking; *ludibrium*, laughing stock]

—◄○►—

fortunophobia
fear of your numbers coming up on the lottery if you don't play

This is a cruel phobia. As the name suggests (**fortunophobia** means, literally, the fear of luck, not, as is often mistakenly reported, fear of your fortune), there is only one surefire way of treating this one and that is with a prescription which reads: 'Take £1, each week, to the lottery shop.'* There really is no other hope. You could go cold turkey and bravely refuse to play the numbers you've had for the last ten years, which, because they are based on a strange algorithm of your family's birthdays, are ingrained in your brain. Within one week,

* The strain *fortunophobia bihebdomas* is rare but not unknown. This strikes not only on Saturdays but also renders the victim mildly jibbering on Wednesdays too. Alan Deddicoat touches on it briefly in his book *Voice of the Balls – The Stagedoor Stories* (Voxpop Press, 2000).

you might be cured. Of course, you might also be an alcoholic barfly, tumbler in hand, regaling any drinker who will listen with the story of 'the week you didn't play'. Ouch. Tough one.

[orig. der.: *fortuna*, luck; *bihebdomas*, twice weekly]

---

frigensophobia
fear of using your mobile

Not to be confused with **tinniphobia** (q.v.), this translates as fear of frying, hence its nickname: 'Chinese aerophobia'. **Frigensophobes** fear that a mobile might be frying their brain. Sometimes, as a result, they will refuse to own a mobile phone; if they are under thirty, this means they soon become social outcasts. More commonly, though, they will adopt unnerving ways of negating the frying effects: holding the phone a foot away from their ear, thus rendering it useless; or, rarely, insisting on using their mobile's speakerphone, so making their public calls doubly annoying, if a little more entertaining.

[orig. der.: *frigere*, to fry]

---

fronsophobia
fear of making tea

The author is perfectly prepared to accept that he has the only known case of **fronsophobia**; nevertheless, he would prefer it to be documented along with every other modern phobia. **Fronsophobia** starts in youth, often triggered by family get-togethers. Being asked to make tea for up to twenty Yorkshire relatives is often enough to bring on a **fronsophobic** attack. Specific requests – Mollie likes it straight from the pot; don't leave Madge and Sheila's in to stew; not too much milk for Pat – are the key to inducing a lifelong phobia and turning the sufferer a seasoned coffee-drinker. There is one strain of **fronsophobia** which *is* universal, however, and that is *fronsophobia fructus*, a fear of fruit or herb teas. Sufferers would love to drink these teas, for their healthy properties, but they are nervous of doing so. They know fruit tea to be the porn of the tea world – all promise and you certainly don't feel any better afterwards. They also know that manufacturers are able to produce a deep, fruity smell on the nose which somehow translates into a taste of hot water on the tongue. Genius.

[orig. der.: *frons*, leaves; *fructus*, fruit]

—<o>—

fucuphobia
fear of make-up counter assistants

Fucuphobes secretly believe that David Dickinson must have fathered all the world's make-up counter assistants. Walking through department stores, sufferers speed up when navigating the girls of Planet Orange, not only for fear – like you and I – of being sprayed by this week's scent (usually named after an NFT foreign film season), but also because they simply *fear* the staff. They feel uneasy around women who appear to have drunk years' worth of Sunny Delight and who are dressed as a cross between an air hostess and a ward orderly. What **fucophobes** fear most, however, are the Stepford smiles, those wide, toothy grins that make-up counter assistants seem to don merely to prove that their facial muscles still work under the strain of their warpaint.

[orig. der.: *fucatum*, painted]

genviaphobia
fear of street pollsters

Genviaphobia sufferers split into two distinct groups: those who fear pollsters and those who fear charity workers. The second group, sufferers of *genviaphobia pauper*, is by far the more numerous and splits into two again: those who fear charity-tin shakers and those who fear charity clipboard workers. Sufferers who fear tin-shakers are encouraged to learn the Oxtrot – originally the 'Oxfam Foxtrot' – a speedy little dance in which the person looks askance and neatly skips to the other side of the road. Amazingly, the clipboard-fearing group splits into two again: those who fear charity clipboarders because they don't want to part with their money, and those who fear them because they know they will not be able to refuse. Members of this last category know that, if they don't cross the road quickly, they will very soon have signed over the deeds to their house. They are the same people who regularly give money to drunks in the street, presuming that 'spare us £1 for Thunderbird' has something to do with Lady Penelope.

[orig. der.: *gens*, tribe; *via*, street; *pauper*, poor]

graphicoitophobia
fear of sex because one's willy is too small

It is worth pointing out that this is not simply fear of sex. This is fear of sex – that's the *coito* bit – for a reason, that reason being your willy is too small (that's the *graph* bit, from *graphium*, meaning pencil). For a true **graphicoitophobe**, sex is something akin to throwing a sausage into the Albert Hall. Symptoms include a devotion to *Star Trek*, an interest in IT and celibacy. First identified by Catullus in 64 BC and famously noted in his poem 'Tomaculum bracae':

> My toga remains placid, my trousers a
>   museum,
> my shrimp-like spear is flaccid, when
>   thrown in the Coliseum.

Not to be confused with **exiphallophobia** (q.v.).

[orig. der.: *graphium*, pencil; *coitus*, joining together]

gyrosaccophobia
fear of baggage-retrieval systems

Gyrosaccophobia is three fears in one. Normal **gyrosaccophobes** fear that their luggage will not appear. What constitutes no more than a momentary irk for most is, to them, a permanent state of mind. *We* feel it, for a moment, just before our bags tumble like an overweight ballet dancer down the slope and on to the conveyor belt. For a **gyrosaccophobe**, it often starts before check-in at the other end: will my luggage ever come back? There are two more forms of **gyrosaccophobia**. Some sufferers fear that their luggage is not up to scratch. It is neither state of the art Samsonite nor old enough to give it that tincture of ageing, aristocratic chic. It's just crap. And they are ashamed. Ever since their mothers sent them to school in non-standard-issue PE pumps – a slightly different colour to everyone else's – they have felt this way. Much more common is *gyrosaccophobia proterva*: fear of coming forward when your baggage, whether up to scratch or not, comes along. These poor, shy, retiring folk simply fear their moment in the sun, seemingly unaware that they are merely stepping forward to pick up a bag, not to claim an Oscar. Very often they are to be found in the coffee bar, nursing a latte, and staring over the balcony at that last, sad case going round and round on its own.

[orig. der.: *gyrus*, circle; *saccus*, bag; *proterve*, boldly]

---

halitophobia
fear that one's breath smells

This is one of those fears that tends to go untreated, mainly because sufferers do not want to admit to it. Symptoms include a constant cupping of the hand over the mouth, followed by a sharp exhalation of breath, often prior to a date. Some sufferers permanently mumble – the knock-on effect of trying to talk without opening their mouth too wide. Many display an exaggerated love of mints. **Halitophobes** often fear the fact that everybody might *know* they have bad breath more than the fact that they *have* bad breath. The **halitophobe** notices that, when people talk to them, they look them in the eye, yet the other person's face points just to their left or right. Odd that. Ironically, when a **halitophobe** detects bad breath in others, they do not tell them.

[orig. der.: *halitus*, breath]

hebdomophobia
fear of Sunday evenings

Many modern phobias lose their social taboo only when championed or brought into the open by somebody in the public eye. **Hebdomophobia** is one such disease, made acceptable when Winston Churchill talked of his 'black dog'. For most, **hebdomophobia** stems from their childhood, when their parents took a post-Sunday roast snooze in front of a black and white *Miss Marple*. With the ice-cream man already having been and the idea of playing football against the wall beginning to lose its appeal, all that remained of the day was, well, the remains of the day: perhaps a BBC adaptation of a famous book, made on a budget of £3, a dark night drawing in, or simply thoughts of Monday morning. This is how **hebdomophobia** starts and, no matter what the lifestyle, it can return at any time, especially since the arrival of Aled Jones on *Songs of Praise*.

[orig. der.: *hebdomas*, terminal point of the week]

◄○►

holuphobia
fear of going gaga

Not surprisingly, most **holuphobes** are in their late forties and fifties, the age at which they first begin to realise the 'ski race of life' is not far off the last phase: the downhill slalom. **Holu-**

phobia is often triggered by a random event – the most common is finding oneself returning the milk to the oven instead of the fridge – which can convince a person that the end is nigh and they will soon be dribbling on to a fluffy, checked blanket with someone asking them what the prime minister is called. **Holuphobes** often take to doing crosswords (or more recently Sudoku) and, in extreme circumstances, join a salsa class. Not to be confused with **holusophobia** (q.v.)

[orig. der.: *holus*, vegetable]

—◦—

holusophobia
fear of vegetables

This disease usually starts in childhood and is often triggered by an incident during which a youngster is made to eat an entire plate of green-coloured food. Sometimes this incident can pass without harm. If, however, the vegetables in question are of the genus *holus diabolus* (this includes cabbage, turnip, swede, etc.), the child may be left with a long-term, albeit potentially curable, case of **holusophobia**. (If the vegetable is of the genus *diabolus maximus* – i.e. sprouts – the disease will be uncurable and, in some instances, can ruin the Christmas season for life). Amazingly, **holusophobia** does not prevent a person from turning vegetarian. Several cases have been reported, often of students who appear to survive on a diet of chips (potatoes are not classed as vegetables to most **holusophobes**), beans and toast.

[orig. der.: *holus*, vegetable; *diabolus*, devil]

-◁◦▷-

hydraphobia
fear of the corporate

Nothing to do with fear of water, **hydraphobia** takes its name from the hydra, meaning a many-headed beast. **Hydraphobes** fear *all* things corporate. They tend to be shareless, often **nomenophobic** (q.v.) and, occasionally, activists who would rather eat their own pan-fried stool than dine at McDonalds. They tend to roll their own. As with vegetarianism, though, **hydraphobia** tends to breed watered-down versions of itself. Just as some vegetarians are prepared to eat fish or, in some cases, cows that died in their sleep, so many **hydraphobes** are actually experiencing hydrophabia c.r.o.e.* This allows the sufferer to carp on, at length, about evil multinationals and the loss of corner shops, while at the same time sporting Nike trainers as they surf for porn on AOL.

[orig. der.: *hydra*, serpent; *c.r.o.e. = *cuius rei optio est*, optional]

ianuarphobia
fear of january

As Betjeman[†] said in his poem, 'Christmas in the Remove':

[†]Keith Betjeman, 1965–

Christmas is upon us, the boys are playing
   rugger,
Enjoy it fast, it will not last – and January's
   a bugger.

Many **ianuarphobes** will attest to the fact that
they were reading these lines at school when it
first dawned on them that they might have the
disease. **Ianuarphobes** envy the tortoise its hiber-
nation because of January's essential, post-
Christmas hardship, and would actually prefer
an eleven-month year. Sufferers are easily spotted
by their sandwich boxes, which they bring to
work with ever more makeshift contents. (The
'January Salad', as it is known, is in fact not a
salad at all, but last night's pasta, eaten cold.)
Therapists say the ideal treatment for this fear
is a long break, somewhere sunny, an irony not
lost on the millions of sufferers who can hardly
afford to get into work in this grisly, grey, God-
forsaken month.

[orig. der.: *Ianuarius*, January]

idemophobia
fear of turning up in the same outfit
as someone else

This is almost entirely a female fear. It is also
much more common the higher up the social
ladder you go. (Well, when you think about it,
turning up wearing the same Top Shop jeans as
your friend will hardly curdle the atmosphere at
a Yates's Wine Lodge). It is also very often a
celebrity fear, ever since magazines like *Heat* and
Hello! took to 'outing' famous types who dared,
inadvertently, to show up looking like Hergé's
Thomson and Thompson. Therapists say **idemo-
phobia** is very hard to treat as there appears to
be a strange, unwritten rule which states that
clothes cannot be a) duplicated by anyone else,
nor b) worn more than once by the same person.
As comedian Jack Dee once remarked, this
phobia does not have a real-life equivalent.
Policemen, for example, don't ring around ahead
of work, asking, 'Hey, you're not wearing a light
blue shirt and flat shoes, are you? You are?
Damn.'

[orig. der.: *idem*, same]

illenomophobia
fear of a certain name

Let me help non-sufferers to understand this fear. Imagine you are being set up with a friend of a friend. They give you the lowdown on him: 'He's handsome' – good. 'He's rich but not pompous with it' – great. 'He's got a great sense of humour' – fab, sounds perfect. 'And he's called Keith.' Oh . . . right. What's the problem? You are an **illenomophobe**, that's what. You fear a certain name – not *necessarily* Keith (although, for a huge proportion of sufferers, for some reason, it *is* Keith). The reason, as any **illenomophobe** will say, is that 'it's not a good name for me'. Symptoms include the aforesaid snap judgements, often arrived at even in the face of conflicting evidence. This can extend beyond simple friendships to work and business dealings, too. I knew one **illenomophobe** who was sinking under six feet of water and in desperate need of a plumber. Everyone he tried had been called out to the recent Maidenhead tsunami. As he craned his neck in the last air-pocket at the top of the attic, he finally got hold of someone willing to come out. 'Just look out for my van saying "Keith's Plumbing",' the white knight said. Ah! . . . thought my friend.

They never did find the body.

[orig. der.: *ille*, that; *nomen*, name]

—◦—

illerogophobia
fear of the unanswerable questions

It should be pointed out, early on, that the unanswerable questions concerning us here are not
the great questions such as what is the meaning
of life, is there a god, or when will I, will I be
famous? No. **Illerogophobia** is the fear of questions which purport to be sincere but are, in fact,
mere verbal window-dressing – i.e. rhetorical bits
of fluff, inserted by either force of habit, the need
to fill a gap or even sheer nerves. Examples of this
kind of question are things like, 'I've got the receipt,
would you like to change it?' The answer to this
is a simple and firm 'no'. Any other answer is unac-
ceptable. **Illerogophobia** strikes most often in part-
nerships, particularly with what doctors call the
'closer' question: 'Does my bum look big in this?'
(see **magnafundaphobia**, q.v.). Again the answer is
simple: no. Do not be tempted to think that there
is an alternative. There isn't. In fact, the more
heartfelt you can make the negative answer sound,

the better – without, of course, resorting to hyper-bole. ('Your bottom is small enough to pass through the eye of a needle, while still leaving room to tow a caravan at either side', for example, would lay you open to a good slapping.) As you can imagine, there are many variants of this disease, but special mention should be made of *illerogophobia amans* – one of the most common – in which the sufferer fears the question, 'Do you love me?'

[orig. der.: *ille*, that; *rogare*, to question]

---

imitorphobia
fear of talking to someone in their accent

A rare yet potentially life-saving phobia, which can help both the sufferers – to escape severe bodily harm – and their acquaintances – to escape general bewilderment. For reasons unknown to themselves – and still not fully understood by therapists – an **imitorphobe** will become desperate to adopt the accent of the person to whom they are talking. If they succumb, the situation is only retrievable on odd occasions – they may be speaking to a Irish priest, for example, who immediately forgives them. In 99 per cent of cases, however, the **imitorphobe** is not so lucky. They may be talking to a supe-rior at work, a potential lover, or, and this is a little more tricky, a member of an Italian organ-ised crime family. It is often rumoured that Stephen Hawking's secretary is a **imitorphobe**, which would be cruel if true, although it has never been confirmed. Rarer still is *imitorphobia mora*, in which the sufferer fears they are about to adopt the glaring speech impediment of their conversa-tion partner. High-profile sufferers include Roy Hattersley's PA and Granville in *Open All Hours*. For useful further reading, try *Impediment? My Rs!* (Tonguetwister Publishing, 2002), written by reformed *imitorphobia mora* sufferer Jane Goldman (wife of Jonathan Ross).

[orig. der.: *imitari*, to imitate; *mora*, hindrance]

–◁◦▷–

inanophobia
fear of being put on hold

Inanophobes do not fear call centres (see **coetuser-mophobia**), nor being *left* on hold (see **depocon-chobia** (Davey's). They fear just being put on hold. For them, 'hold' is an empty, soulless place, something like Slough. They often develop quicker-than-average speech patterns, frequently shouting out 'No, don't put me on . . .' at the top of their voices before meekly and dejectedly whispering the word 'hold' when they realise they are already there. In the great void. They tremble at the phrase, 'Your call is important to us.'

[orig. der.: *inanitas*, empty space]

—◦—

incarmophobia
fear of starting a communal song

In every stadium of, say, 85,000 people, scientists reckon there are some 84,995 **incarmophobes**. That means that, statistically, you and I are much more likely to be **incarmophobic** than not. I know I am. **Incarmophobes** cannot understand how their friends are able suddenly to get thousands of people singing along with their new chant – especially considering a) they've never heard the words before, and b) the subject matter is a risky tale of the sexual proclivities of Posh and Becks. Not to mention c) that their friend could not be sure these 85,000 folk would suddenly know the tune to Verdi's *La Traviata*. Worst of all, for the **incarmophobe,** is the sheer spunk it takes to shout, amidst a crowd of your tattooed, half-cut peers, 'Hey, lads, forget pissing into that guy's pocket, try this one,' and then lead a chorus on your own. Do you hand round song sheets? What? An **incarmophobe** cannot work it out. *Incarmophobia undabracchia* is the similar but distinct fear of starting a Mexican wave, a particularly virulent strain of the disease wherein the sufferer longs for but at the same time fears the moment at which they jump to their feet and wave both arms in the air, in an attempt to get the crowd to follow suit. Sometimes hard to tell apart from Tourette's.

[orig. der.: *instituere*, to start; *carmen*, song; *unda*, wave; *bracchium*, arm]

―◦―

indensophobia
fear that you have something stuck in your teeth

The author is not aware of any other phobia that requires people to cure themselves before they know they have contracted it. That is, you only know you are a sufferer once you check to make sure you're not. It's like this. You suffer from *indensophobia prima*, fearing that you might have something stuck in your teeth. But you are at a rather posh twin-set and pearls do. You've tried smiling into your wineglass to see the reflection. You tried motioning to your partner and giving them a quick, over-expansive smile, but they just thought you were a) randy, b) drunk, or c) both. So you just go for it and stick your fingers in your mouth. There is *no* rotting Chinese leaf there, left over from the starter. You are cured. Similar is the fear of having had a sign stuck on your back, most commonly suffered by teachers. The minute you check, you're cured. It's known to therapists as the 'Rod Stewart Principle': by the time you realise what you have, you've haven't got it.

[orig. der.: *dens*, tooth]

infansermophobia
fear that one's small child will hang up
during a critical telephone conversation

> Mum: Who was that on the phone, sweet-
> heart?
> Child: It was Daddy – he was trapped down
> a mineshaft with only twenty minutes
> of oxygen left.
> Mum: Where's the phone now, darling?
> Child: Erm . . .
> Mum: Oh, Toby, you haven't buried it in the
> garden again, have you? You rascal!'

Thankfully, your conversation is probably never
going to be *that* critical. But the **infansermo-
phobe** might perceive it as such. They fear that
they have such a thin, thread-like grip on the
conversation that, at any point, they might be
cut off and hidden in the top floor of a doll's
house. *Now, how will they get a lift from the
station?* Signs of **infansermophobia** include
repeating the following conversation, word for
word, on the bus:

'Hello, Daisy, it's Daddy . . . Daisy darling
. . . Daisy . . . oh hello, Daisy darling, is
Mummy there, darling . . . oh, you're in

the toy room . . . can you – hello, Daisy, darling . . . Daisy . . . Daisy darling, pick up the phone . . . pick up the phone, sweetheart . . . DAISY . . . HELLO . . . CAN ANYBODY HEAR ME? . . . I THINK I'M ON THE MANTELPIECE.

[orig. der.: *infans*, child; *sermo*, conversation]

―◦―

insistophobia
fear of parking

One of the few phobias that is more female than male (but only just, at 54–46 per cent). The phobia takes its name from the Latin word for 'coming to a stop'. Intriguingly, the same word can also mean to press on or to continue, so perhaps therein lies the problem. To an **insistophobe**, parking a bubble car in the Grand Canyon would be a problem, hence the only reason many choose to upgrade their car is to obtain the new parking sensors, which beep when you are nearing another motor. For **insistophobes**, it is not that they *can't* do it. Very often, once, they could. It's just that, at some point – only once, perhaps – they didn't do it, and, from then on, it didn't matter whether they could or they couldn't: they simply didn't *believe* that they could. Add in a potential tight space, a busy road and a line of workmen sat watching whilst eating their lunch, and you have a recipe for a breakdown. Often literally. **Insistophobes** tend not to take their cars when they can help it, preferring to use public transport. They also tend to love country fêtes, where parking is in a field, and often dream of stock-car racing while driving backwards, looking over their shoulder. The old joke about why women can't park has gone out of fashion somewhat, ever since it was learned that this was what sparked the famous domestic argument in the Bobbitt household.

[orig. der.: *insistere*, to halt]

—◦—

instratophobia
fear of getting back out there

This very common fear gets its name from the Latin phrase 'to get back in the saddle' (*stratum* = saddle) and, with divorce rates ever on the increase, the number of **instratophobes** continues to grow. Symptoms often start with a penchant for supermarket dinners for one. Sufferers can often find that they are much more comfortable wearing a cardigan out of the house. Chronic **instratophobes** will know virtually every line of *When Harry Met Sally*. Sufferers tend to redefine their social parameters, too. Speed dating, for example, no longer means meeting up with several people in one organised night. It means going out with someone new for dinner but doing a runner out of sheer nerves before the main course has arrived.

[orig. der.: *in*, in; *stratum*, saddle]

―◄◌►―

invimedicophobia
fear of going to the doctor

Not connected at all to **discimedicophobia** (q.v.), **invimedicophobia** is largely a male disease, What **invimedicophobes** fear is fear itself. What *might* be wrong with them. Why is this cough taking so long to shake? Could be bronchitis. Could be scurvy. As a result, they don't go to the doc's. Symptoms include a tendency to chant the well-known mantra 'can't afford the time off work, can't afford the time off work', or the increasingly popular 'I mean, why don't these people work on a Saturday any more, for heaven's sake?' **Invimedicophobia** is invariably cured by partners, who get so sick of the bleating that they book the appointment themselves. After visiting the doctor, of course, sufferers invariably discover they have man-flu and so go into mourning for ten days, taking care to update their will, just in case.

[orig. der.: *invenire*, to discover; *medicus*, doctor]

--<o>--

ipsoblivophobia
fear that one will one day think it's a good idea to . . .

This is a so-called 'friendly fear', a sort of Yakult of the phobia world. The word derives from the latin *ipse*, meaning self, and *oblivium*, meaning forgetfulness. So, an **ipsoblivophobe** fears they will literally forget themselves. In practice, what this means is that they fear, for example, that they might one day think it a good idea to . . . take up golf (*ipsoblivophobia pargloba*). Or they might think it a good idea to . . . sport a moustache (*ipsoblivophobia nascappilia*). These are two of the most common forms. If people did not have these phobias, there would be many more plus-fours in the world, not to mention enough Jason King look-alikes to fill a town the size of Kettering. Some **ispsoblivophobes** become so anxious that they deposit letters with their solicitors marked 'only to be opened in the event of my . . . ironing my jeans', for example (*ipsoblivophobia linea*). Better to be safe than sad. Other major strains include: *ipsoblivophobia unasola* – fear that you will one day think it's a good idea to . . . live in a bungalow; *ipsoblivophobia spumalacta* – fear that you will one day think it's a good idea to . . . drink Bailey's; and *ipsoblivophobia aestavina* – fear that you will one day think it's a good idea to . . . watch *Last of the Summer Wine*.

[orig. der.: *ipse*, self; *oblivium*, forgetfulness]

—◦—

lacvasophobia
fear of the milk carton

It may seem incomprehensible to most of us, but some people do develop a fear of milk cartons, so much so that a group lawsuit is being prepared in Holland on behalf of twenty-seven people who all started opening milk in the sixties and who say they were not given enough information on the intrinsic dangers of doing so (central to the case is the premise that the instructions, re 'pull back wings', etc., appeared far too late for them to do anything about their problem – by then some of them were on three Tetra Paks a day, all of them ruined). The results of that test case will not be known until next year but the ramifications, particularly for **lacvasophobes**, could be crucial. The majority of **lacvasophobes** fear opening milk cartons because they have been so unsuccessful at it in the past. Newer cartons, with their plastic ring-pulls, have done little to reduce the numbers of people calling the 'No Use Crying . . .' helpline. Even more recent plastic bottles with their cruel, hidden ring-pulls under the cap, are actually thought to have turned yet more people **lacvasophobic**. A rare but particular type of sufferer, the *lacvasophobe olidus*, does not strictly speaking fear the milk carton, but its contents – principally because they think the milk may have gone sour. These people are easily identified by the fact that they often drink their tea or coffee black, they frequently have their nose in a milk bottle/carton, or they are always mumbling phrases like, 'Mmm, I think it's on the turn.'

[orig. der.: *lac*, milk; *vas*, vessel; *olidus*, smelly or rank]

lanxophobia
fear of getting on the scales

Some people never do it. Others do it now and again. These days, though, a large proportion do it rather a lot. As a result, **lanxophobia** is quite common. **Lanxophobes** have their own way of moving. It stems from the belief that, while the camera never lies, the scales can be made to tell the odd porky (or should that be porker?). So they creep ballet-like on to the scales with one pointed toe, and prod them up and down. Once aboard, they slink to the very edges, or lean as far sideways as they can without overbalancing, all in genuine fear of what the scales may say. Other symptoms include peeping through their clenched fingers at the read-out, as if watching their worst nightmare horror movie. Which, in many ways, they are.

[orig. der.: *lanx*, scale]

laudaphobia
fear of fans

Often misconceived as being something to do with stalkers (it isn't), **laudaphobia** is now extremely rare. In an age when students can now take an A level in fame, **laudaphobia** is almost unheard of. In the rare event that therapists do come across a celebrity in need of fan rehab, they recommend Freud's inverse recognition technique, in which the celeb approaches the fan with the words: 'Excuse me, but . . . haven't you seen me somewhere on television?' This can get them back on the road to true vanity in no time, from where a relaxingly paranoid state of egomania cannot be far away.

[orig. der.: *laudare*, to praise]

◄○►

maginvalophobia
fear of being visited by an MP in hospital

Thankfully rare, **maginvalophobes** are astonishing people. They fear the thought of being involved in a nasty train crash *less* than being visited by a beaming MP later in hospital. A recurring nightmare amongst many **maginvalophobes** is being totally bandaged from head to toe, unable to speak, and then seeing Margaret Thatcher inching round the curtain saying, 'We are a visitor.'

[orig. der.: *magistratus*, politician; *valetudinarium*, hospital]

---

magnafundaphobia
fear that one's bum looks big in this

An almost entirely female affliction which can manifest itself not only in a clothes shop changing-room but also whilst passing virtually any full-length mirror. Much is now being done to break the taboo on talking about the proportions of the female arse, particularly by the new crop of self-help groups which have popped up following Davina McCall's ground-breaking appearances on *Big Brother*. A number of self-help groups have sprung up recently, including Seats of Learning, Buns to You and 'It's the Size of a Small Country and I'm Proud' Community Care Association, et al. Online websites and repeats of *The Fast Show* are helping, too.

[orig. der.: *magnus*, large; *fundus*, bottom]

---

magnufraterphobia
fear of reality television

Literally, 'fear of big brother'. Again, one of the friendly fears which doctors now think is the body's way of keeping the brain active. Those who inadvertently cure themselves of this fear often display a propensity to refer to dates in weeks (week 1, week 2, etc.), to smile and say, 'Aww . . . Davina!' every time they see her, and, in chronic cases, to realise suddenly that they have spent the last forty-two minutes watching four people asleep in a room with the lights out. And enjoyed it. If you know anyone in this post-phobic state, doctors say you should not approach as it is dangerous to wake them.

[orig. der.: *magnus*, big; *frater*, brother]

--◦--

malcantophobia
fear of singing

As the name suggests, **malcantophobes** do not generally fear singing, but singing badly. It has famously afflicted a small minority of high-profile people: John Redwood, World Cup footballers, Victoria Beckham, etc. Most sufferers, though, fear singing the wrong section (*malcantophobia pars*), or, worse still, singing on after everyone has stopped (*malcantophobia videpenis*). First things first. *Malcantophobia pars* sufferers overwhelmingly develop their fear in school and it is often born out of having paid insufficient attention. *Videpenis* patients deserve more sympathy as, like Tourette's, the chief symptom of their malaise can appear outwardly comical. They fear continuing a song after it has finished because nature has not provided them with the gene which senses that singing is about to cease. The majority of *videpenis* sufferers tend to have their first attack during the song 'For he's a jolly good fellow', often adding a whole line on the end when everyone else has finished before being able to pull up. There is one other, rarer form of the disease, *malcantophobia ecclesia*, which is unique to churches. Here, sufferers have no fear of anything to do with words – no matter how obscure the hymn, the words are there in front of them, in the hymnbook. Instead, they panic about lack of knowledge of the *tune*. They feel trapped, desperate to join in but keen, too, not to appear a growler. In the end, they tend to opt for simply lowering the volume, but, alas, their twelve-tone version of the tune has usually been clocked.

[orig. der.: *male*, badly; *cantare*, to sing; *pars*, part; *videre*, to appear; *penis*, a dick]

◄○►

malolidophobia
fear that one smells but has never been told

This is one of the 'Compton's Spiral' series of phobias, so named after the person who first discovered it. The spiral is said to represent eternity, as once you have this fear there is little chance of you ever being cured – mainly because a) you will never be prepared to admit to anyone that you have it, and b) if you ever did, you then wouldn't believe others if they said there was no problem. You are in Compton's Spiral. Symptoms include compulsive sniffing of one's own armpits, the ability to clear the top deck of a bus in seconds, and a washing regime that would put Lady Macbeth to shame. Compton did identify one instance in which sufferers can extricate themselves from the spiral – if the **malolidophobe** were to be in a long-term relationship, where they felt able not only to ask but to trust the answer of a very close partner. Of course, cruelly, this will never happen.

[orig. der.: *male*, badly; *olidus*, smelly or rank]

-◄o►-

malventophobia
fear that one's farts smell worse than anyone else's

Not a common fear by any standards but, nonetheless, a debilitating one – and, to be fair, generally a clandestine one. **Malventophobes** cannot easily spark up a conversation on the subject ('Another sandwich, Auntie Elsie? By the way, on a scale of one to ten . . .'), and some therapists have refused to accept them on to their books – not because they don't take it seriously, but because the room might be left stale for the next client. Ironically, due to the underground nature of this phobia, many **malventophobes** will never be able to receive the news that their fear is groundless. Another branch of the disease is *malventophobia stercus*, covering that area of human waste normally handled by Armitage Shanks and Co. Sufferers often purchase one of those supposedly humorous signs that say 'I'd give it 10 minutes'. Often with good reason. Let's leave it there, shall we?

[orig. der.: *male*, badly; *ventus*, wind; *stercus*, excrement]

malvocophobia
fear of using the wrong words

Most of us have at some point suffered a little twinge of regret at failing to reach for the correct word. This is not **malvocophobia**. **Malvocophobia** manifests itself *before* the words have been uttered and is often a sign that the person is also **alia-callophobic** (q.v.) too. **Malvos** (slang) have a permanent dread of using words they don't know the meaning of and, hence, their favourite person in *Friends* is Joey. (There is a rare form, *malvo-cophobia aversa*, which works in reverse. *Aversa* sufferers think things like, 'Did I just say vicar-iously? Was it right? Do I really know what means? Damn, I said jejune again. Must look it up when I get home. Don't think anyone noticed.') In its original form, **malvocophobia** can be cured, although this does not mean, as some believe, that the subject can suddenly use long, flashy words and know what their meaning is. It simply means that they no longer have the fear. High-profile ex-**malvocophobes** include Hylda Baker, John Prescott and President Bush. Increasingly common, especially in the 18–30 age bracket, is *malvocophobia aliena*, where a person has a fear of other people using words he or she doesn't know the meaning of. In practice, the *aliena* sufferer has then to decide which way to go. 'She just said she never did see eye to eye with *monandry*. What the hell does *monandry* mean? Oh sod it. Let's try this: "Neither do I – his paintings are so one-dimensional, aren't they?"'

[orig. der.: *male*, bad; *vocabulum*, vocabulary; *aversus*, backwards; *alienus*, strange]

-◄◦►-

manepostophobia
fear of having done something awful whilst drunk

Anyone who has ever woken up and not quite been able to remember the drunken events of the night before can claim to have suffered from **manepostophobia**. Taken from the the ancient Latin, 'morning-after disease' covers a host of ailments from waking up with a traffic cone in your bed, to the much more interesting, if slightly more dangerous, waking up with a traffic warden in your bed. This wide-ranging phobia also takes in drunken arguments that your spouse assures you will mean certain friends never inviting you round to dinner again, as well as the more modern strain: getting a phone call from a friend to say you've just appeared on *The World's Naughtiest*

CCTV Footage with your wedding tackle hanging out, singing 'Mule Train', using your briefcase as a tray. **Manepostophobes**, one and all.

[orig. der.: *mane*, morning; *post*, after]

◄◦►

materphobia
fear of one's mother

Show me a man who has ever admitted to being a **materphobe**. Quite. And yet, according to the most recent figures available (2004), there are over 50,000 registered **materphobes** in Europe, and 44,000 in Italy alone. **Materphobes** hide their illness well. They often marry, have children and even hold down responsible jobs, mostly in the civil service. Give-aways include a reluctance – despite their wife's requests – to ask their mother to refrain from birching her grandchildren, a high phone bill (**materphobes** cannot abide accusations of not calling), and a disproportionate love of the smell of home-baking and aprons. The film *Psycho* works on so many more levels for a **materphobe**. Not to be confused with **socruphobia** (q.v.).

[orig. der.: *mater*, mother]

―◦―

medicamerophobia
fear of doctors' waiting rooms

Another of the friendly fears, this is a totally understandable fear of the coughing, spluttering, unhealthy bunch of loafers you see in these cold, draughty rooms (and that includes yourself, of course). Specific strains include *medicamera-phobia crepundia*, generally suffered by mothers, which is the fear that those rather rancid-looking, half-chewed toys may somehow have become impregnated with the whooping cough virus (*medicameraphobia lectia* sufferers feel the same about the magazines). A tiny number suffer *medicameraphobia libellus*, where a patient cannot bear to reread the dull posters in doctors' waiting rooms in case they gradually convince themselves they have all the symptoms of all the diseases on all the posters in the room. Many people are chonic *medicameraphobia animadvertia* sufferers. These strange folk have a phobia of being spotted in the doctor's waiting room, for fear that their particular ailment might be outed (symptoms include nightmares from which they are awoken with a shout, from across the street, of 'Hey, Keith, how's the thrush?') Finally, a rare and tiny proportion of people have *medicameraphobia donaria*, a fear of donating their old magazines to the doctor's waiting room in case they are not highbrow enough (now totally eradicated amongst subscribers to *Interiors*, *Horse and Hound* and *Reader's Digest*).

[orig. der.: *medicus*, doctor; *camera*, room; *crepundia*, baby's toy; *lectio*, reading; *libellus*, notice; *animadvertere*, to observe; *donarium*, offering]

◄○►

molliphobia
fear of not being able to get it up

Molliphobia is similar in origin to **vencelerphobia** (q.v.) but is not restricted only to actual times of passion. **Molliphobes** tend to suffer attacks in the cab from the restaurant after a meal, or at home, when their partner has uttered those magic words, 'I'm going up, you won't be long, will you?' For those suffering in the cab, it has been proven that coffee is often a trigger word for a **molliphobic** attack. The evening may have gone well, and indeed the journey home, too. But when coffee is mentioned – usually within the question, 'Would you like to come up for coffee?' – all hell breaks loose. Very often, though, the **molliphobe** will not even get to this stage of the evening: their fears get the better of them and coffee is never offered – or if it is, it is coffee and not 'coffee' – The scientific boundaries for **molliphobia** were only laid down as late as 1987, by Bruce Stirling (working out of the University of Geelong, formerly Balliang Institute). It was he who established the so-called 'Belle Test': if, in lab conditions (a gents' toilet is permissible), a person can think of Catherine Deneuve in *Belle de Jour* without at least a semi, they will probably, at some point in their life, become or have been **molliphobic**. There is no known cure for **molliphobia** beyond celibacy.

[orig. der.: *mollis*, soft]

◆◇◆

musaurophobia
fear of people in oversized headphones

It may come as something of a shock to members of the younger generation, but the act of walking along one of the Queen's highways while wearing a pair of oversized headphones can be very distressing to some. **Musaurophobes** (the name is thought to come from a clandestine group of music lovers in fifth-century Ireland, who took to wearing 'mouse ears' when they met) are not afraid of headphones per se. Micro- and Walkman-sized headphones do not present them with a problem. Instead, they fear the folk who wear headphones that would be more at home in a recording studio or the isolation booth on 'Mr and Mrs'. These tend to be DJs, computer nerds and Xfm listeners, who appear totally unaware that many people think they are the soundman who has become separated from his television crew. **Musauro-phobes** have often cited 'people in gas masks during the war' as a recurring nightmare, after having spotted a Mickey Mouse (the self-help name for a person in oversized headphones). Wearers of said equipment often sport cases for carrying vinyl records or retro duffle-coats.

[orig. der.: *mus*, mouse; *auris*, ear]

---

nihilophobia
fear of nothing

Before you close the book, I should say that fear of nothing is not the same as having no fears. **Nihilophobia** attacks people young and old, very often from distinct social groupings. For example, many toddlers – just around the onset of the 'terrible twos' – fear nothing and, though parents often expect the worst, that's fine. The minute they land on their nose having jumped off the top of their Tomy garage, they will be cured. Drunks, however, are a different kettle of fish. The word **nihilophobia** was made for them, as they willingly climb lampposts, walk on high, thin walls, or attempt to stop traffic with their face. Sundays tend to cure **nihilophobes** for a period of six days, after which symptoms recur. A rarer but well-publicised form, *nihilophobia saxa*, tends only to afflict tattooed rock stars. In its mildest form, it can lead to them diving off the stage into crowds of fans, but on a bad night they might take their Roller with them when they go swimming.

[orig. der.: *nihil*, nothing; *saxa*, rock]

—◦—

nimitempophobia
fear of overstaying one's welcome

Most folk never give their unknown, innate *welcome meter* a thought. The same body clock that makes them wake up at 7 a.m. on Sundays, regardless of the fact that they long to lie in, will also set what's called an 'eyebrow' alarm, common in many social occasions. When this goes off – the eyes widen, the eyebrows rise – they throw their partner a look and, within a decent interval, they are on the backseat of a cab, heading home. **Nimitempophobes**, on the other hand, have lost the ability to set their own body alarms. As a result, within minutes of starting dessert at a dinner party, they are on edge and their tic-tac mechanism makes them look like Stevie Wonder, midsong. Any reference to time is seized upon as if their host had turned on the sprinklers and sent in Dobermanns; often sufferers are out of the door without having retrieved their coats. Sometimes, of course, drink can turn the **nimitempophobe** into the exact opposite: an **anti-nimitempophobe**. These people are easily identified. They are the ones who, at 3.20 a.m., when one of the two hosts has already gone to bed and the other is semaphoring the words 'please die a slow and painful death' at them, suggest cheese and port and another round of Yahtzee.

[orig. der.: *nimis*, too much; *tempus*, time]

-◄○►-

nomenophobia
fear of brands

The appearance of Muji, the unbranded brand, so to speak, set many **nomenophobes** back a few years. Until Muji, sufferers could shun named, branded clothing ('DKNY – Don't Keep Named Yarns' is a common battle-cry of the **nomeno-phobe**) and simply opt for Asda's own if they wanted to venture out in public without looking like a billboard. Then came Muji, though, and suddenly the unnamed brand . . . was a named brand. Catch-22. Therapists had a field day, reporting that many so-called 'cured' **nomenophobes** had re-registered. One of the ironic aspects of this was that many couldn't bear to return to the same shrink, considering them to be a known name themselves and therefore a brand. Incidentally, a cured **nomenophobe** is referred to by a mnemonic taken from the four letters which are placed on the patient's file once the therapist deems them to be signed off and capable of visibly sporting any label: Can Handle All Visuals. Or CHAV.

[orig. der.: *nomen*, name]

◄●►

noninvophobia
fear of not finding things

It may seem an obvious thing to say (certainly to **noninvophobes**), but this is not fear of losing something. Nor of not having something because it *is* lost. It is fear of not finding things. Why did George Bush spend so long searching for weapons of mass destruction? Well, two possible answers: a) there weren't any, or b) he was a **noninvophobe**. If he'd been a girl, the course of history might have been different. Girls tend not to suffer from **noninvophobia**. Men, however, can go back into a room to look for the same thing, over and over again, and never find it. Even if it is staring them in the face. Sufferers talk of a feeling similar to being on *Candid Camera* and sometimes swear a scene has been doctored. Others compare it to a Harry Potter invisibility cloak. Mothers with young children are immune from **noninvophobia** and yet, once the birds have flown the nest, the same women can come down with a deep-seated case of the disease, particularly when it comes to glasses and keys.

[orig. der.: *invenire*, to find]

―◦―

nonmarterophobia
fear of there not being a BBC

This is a modern version of an ancient fear, originating in the era of the Roman forum, when citizens had become used to the public dissemination of information, shouted from podiums on behalf of the senate. Nowadays, it is largely prevalent amongst the so-called 'chattering classes', its chief symptom being a passionate and vehemently argued love of Radio 4. Originally meaning 'fear of no auntie', **nonmarterophobia** is usually spotted in speech patterns. Typical signs of chronic and deep-seated **nonmarterophobia** include sufferers beginning conversations about how they can listen to programmes on Radio 4 which sound bizarre, but within minutes they are hooked. (Some therapists even recognise a separate, merciless strain, *nonmarterophobia hodie*, where patients cannot be more than two minutes away from the voice of John Humphrys and must sleep in until after 9 a.m. on Sundays.) In dire cases, doctors can sign papers to have sufferers 'chipped', a rare operation wherein a small receiver which automatically picks up the shipping forecast is implanted behind the right ear. Bizarrely, hand in hand with **nonmarterophobia** goes a syndrome called WTDP*, which causes an inexplicable compulsion amongst sufferers to attack the very thing they love. Symptoms are mild: writing letters to *The Times*, including the phrase 'a waste of licence-fee money', criticising the governors for rescheduling the start time of CBBC, etc.

[orig. der.: *martertera*, auntie]

---

* Wood and Tree Differentiation Problem – an inability to see the wood for the trees.

novamundaphobia
fear of Americans

With a common image of modern America being
the obese, non-passport-owning invader, the wartime
line of 'overpaid, oversexed and over here' has been
replaced by the more recent 'overweight, over there,
overthrow whoever'. To be fair, **novamundaphobes**
fear this image more than the Americans themselves, who invariably turn out to be charming
when encountered in the queue for the London
Planetarium. A little-known strain of the disease is
novamundaphobia fabula, in which people fear the
unconvincing American accents favoured by BBC
radio drama producers, who seem to cast all
American characters to sound like Foghorn Leghorn.

[orig. der.: *novellus*, new; *mundus*, world; *fabula*,
story]

-<o>-

nuduphobia
fear of being naked

Not to be mistaken for **exuerphobia** (q.v.), this
often potent malaise affects not only the gross
and the ghoulish but also the great and the good.
On an everyday level, sufferers insist on darkness

before changing in front of their partner; prefer to go to bed first; and always bathe with bubbles, so that only their head is exposed. On a celebrity level, it can often result in contract clauses compelling the use of a bottom double for all 'asswork.' *Nuduphobia diutinia* – the same-sex, adult form of the disease – is more common than doctors once thought. It is particularly prevalent in the middle-aged male bracket, where sport is taken up late in life, and where, if wives are known to gossip, showers are an issue. Amongst females it is on the wane, thanks in part to the sterling work done by the Women's Institute calendar.

[orig. der.: *nudus*, naked; *diutinus*, lasting]

—◦—

nullophobia
fear of rejection

Once the world's leading authority on **nullophobia,** Sigmund Volupto stated in 1927 that he had cured over 1,000 **nullophobes**. He went on to add that the number would have been 2,000 if the rest of them could only have brought themselves to ask for an appointment. Even today, fear of rejection is thought to be one of the world's most common phobias, affecting roughly half the population of the UK alone and annoying the hell out of the other half. **Nullophobia** is debilitating. Sufferers consider the disease to be their emotional immune system, protecting them from situations which could see them hurt. In many ways it is an umbrella fear for many of the phobias in this book – **priormotorphobia**, for example (q.v.), and **occupatophobia** (q.v.), to name but two. Interestingly, in much the same way as the Women's Institute play 'Jerusalem' at the beginning of every session, so **nullophobe** self-help groups play videos of the Del Monte advert, screaming wildly as they parrot, '. . . he say yes!'

[orig. der.: *nullus*, no]

---

obsoletophobia
fear that everyone has a better mobile than you

A truly modern fear and one which is increasingly prevalent. At first, **obsoletophobia** merely attacked those who did not have a great handset. Then it singled out those with non-colour graphics. Now it is spreading and knows no bounds. Doctors are predicting a potential epidemic if current trends continue. It's no longer just about the graphics or the camera (wedding photographers now take commissions for weddings where the snaps are taken with their phone). Comments like 'Oh, you can't get E4 on yours, how quaint' can both wound and mystify an **obsoletophobe**. Some sufferers can be seriously hindered in the healing process by their children, too – if your offspring insists you walk seven feet ahead because of that 'iron lung you're carrying', it can hurt.

[orig. der.: *obsoletus*, obsolete]

obsonophobia
fear of checkouts

It is a common misconception that **obsonophobes** fear the people behind the till, or the tills themselves. Not so. Research conducted at the Quur Ching University, near Beijing, now shows irrefutably that **obsonophobes** fear the checkout *speed*. For years, they have been maligned as odd, rude or just downright tight, but now it appears that they simply could not cope with packing their stuff while the checkout person hurled fruit and veg at them as if they were in medieval stocks. Now that the subject has been brought into the open – both by the Beijing research and Dietrich Bach-Öhd's recent book, *Clubcard Generation: The Seven Most Common Habits of the World's Most Successful Shoppers* (transl. Phil Bagges, Life University Press, 2002) which devotes two entire chapters to checkouts, and one of them to self-serve tills – many **obsonophobes** realise they now have common nightmares. One in particular is about being on *The Generation Game*, but set in Sainsbury's, when the conveyor belt goes wrong – this was found to have occurred to around 31 per cent of sufferers (21 per cent even had Brucie at the till). Subsidiary fears have now been identified, too, most notably *obsonophobia sacca*, a fear of not being able to open the plastic bags. Equally common is *obsonophobia sacca fracta*, where patients choose to bag almost every item separately rather than risk trying to walk out of the supermarket only to have their bags split near the cigarette kiosk.

[orig. der.: *obsonare*, to shop; *saccus*, bag; *fractus*, broken]

◄○►

occupatophobia
fear of being 'busied'

'Busy' never used to be an intransitive verb, until mobile phones came along. Now, though, one can 'be busied' – that is, someone can see a name come up on their mobile and choose to press the 'busy' option, thereby sending the call to the answerphone. **Occupatophobes** fear that they didn't just *not get through*. They fear that the other person wasn't just away from their phone. They fear that they are innately tedious creatures and that you consigned them to mobile oblivion, to hear the great Voice of Cell saying, '. . . if you want to re-record your message, press 1 . . . at any time.' Tough one, this. It's incurable, you see. Most doctors will simply say 'Get a life' and tell you to get out. If you refuse to leave it there, and ring to pester for an appointment, well . . . they'll probably busy your calls.

[orig. der.: *occupatus*, busy]

—◦—

ocuviaphobia
fear of making eye contact with someone in the street

Ocuviaphobes fear transitory acknowledgement. They fear it for a number of different reasons. *Ocuviaphobia notus* sufferers fear it due to the situation – perhaps they are in a shop they wouldn't want to own up to being in (envisaging newspaper headlines like 'Local woman found in Poundstretcher'.) Occasionally events disadvantage them – their child may have just projectile-vomited, for example. *Ocuviaphobia collega* is more common and involves fear of making contact with someone because they are a work colleague (or, in the case of teachers, a pupil). Sufferers attest to an initial 'am I spotted?' moment, after which point symptoms include *use of props* – a situation whereby the sufferer shows a heightened attachment to things normally of no interest and proceeds to point them out, mutedly, in the style of a film extra. Other symptoms include the fake walk-past (officially *ambulatio simulare*) at a brisk pace. Occasionally this is the end of an attack, but it can also lead to fake recognition (*cognitio simulare*), where the sufferer is forced to emit over-effusive cries of 'Oh, I didn't see you!', etc. Stilted conversation ensues, in which they gauge whether they got away with it. Chronic sufferers will even try to discern whether their friend attempted a fake walk-past themselves. Cruelly, the subconscious reason for the attack often now kicks in: an inability to remember the person's name. This is often remedied through use of 'gov' or 'squire' or other titles instead of names ('How's . . . er . . . your wife?'). Many leave the scene feeling they got away with it. Statistics show, however, that they rarely do. NB: this is a totally separate fear from **donoculophobia** (q.v.).

[orig. der.: *oculus*, eye; *via*, street; *notus*, known; *collega*, colleague; *ambulatia*, walk; *simulare*, to fake; *cognitio*, recognition]

-<o>-

officinophobia
fear of work

Who hasn't suffered from this at some time? Some folk have it all their lives, poor devils. Only a small minority never get it at all (children, royalty, plumbers, etc.). Indeed, Camelot recently commissioned research which showed that a vast proportion of people who play the lottery are **officinophobes**. Rather than visiting a doctor, most sufferers are diagnosed by their partners or friends, a common trigger being staying in bed until 12 on a weekday. Long-term **officinophobes** will wear their overcoats at work between 4 and 5.30 p.m., with only the hood on, without the arms in – like they did in school when they were 'in the blocks', waiting for the bell to go.

[orig. der.: *officina*, workplace]

‹o›

ostentlorphobia
fear that you are showing your pants

This is one of a number of phobias wherein the male suffers exactly the opposite of the female.

The male version, **ostentlorphobia**, reflects a debilitating worry that the sufferer will show his pants when he bends down. The female version, **non-ostentlorphobia**, afflicts people who fear that they are *not* showing their G-strings above the back of their jeans/skirts when bending down or otherwise. As it has become *de rigueur* that a G-string should be worn at least a foot higher than the waistline these days, **non-ostentlor-phobes** abound – at discos (are they still called discos?), in offices and even on the street. From the Latin *ostentare*, to show, and *lorum*, thong. The first recorded usage is from Seneca's diaries of AD 55:

Dined as guest of Nero.
Rabbit with dates, again.
Drank heartily.
Laughed myself silly when Agrippina inad-
     vertently sported some butt floss almost
     up to her neck.
Home by 11.

[orig. der.: *ostentatio*, showing off; *lorum*, thong]

◄○►

oviphobia
fear of jumping on the bandwagon

Oviphobia is a cruel fear, translating as something like 'fear of sheep'. Ultimately, **oviphobes** become their own worst enemy. They have missed a certain boat – often through no fault of their own – and feel they would be seen as just jumping on the bandwagon were they to sign up now. For example, I know one person who missed the Harry Potter bandwagon. By the time she realised that Harry Potter was actually more than quite good, she was years into the whole Potter gravy train. Having previously said she found nothing in it, she couldn't all of a sudden say, 'Oh I do love the clever puns on names you know . . . Diagon Ally' and screech with laughter. She was late. She had missed the boat. Incidentally, the verb 'to miss the boat' is irregular, you notice. It declines:

I . . . was not a victim of marketing
You . . . missed the boat
He/she . . . jumped on the bandwagon

and so on. As a result, the **oviphobe** goes through life denying themselves something of which they have more than a vague suspicion they might love. New strains of the disease identified within the last ten years include: *oviphobia parvabritan-nia* (*Little Britain*), *oviphobia verba* (texting), *oviphobia farrago* (*Schott's Miscellany*), *ovi-phobia parvacustia* (the Berliner *Guardian*) and *oviphobia occidens* (*The West Wing*).

[orig. der.: *ovis*, sheep]

—◦—

paremusophobia
fear of one's parents' music

This fear is virulent in its early years but does tend to dissipate with age. In their youth, **paremuso-phobes** will walk miles to avoid the strains of their parents' weird and wonderful music. Later on, though, these songs can become nostalgia triggers, capable of transplanting them back to their youth. Perry Como, Jim Reeves, any artist on the Ronco label – these are no longer painful travesties on the ear but glassy-eyed reminders of a finer time, largely in shorts. A long-forgotten parental track on a pub jukebox can stop a person dead in their tracks and take them back to tank tops in an instant. The disease is less prevalent today, partly due to the wider preponderance of earphones, but also because of the sharing of iPod playlists and the seemingly all-embracing music selections of Radio 2. *Paremusophobia exsulia* is a related condition in which the sufferer fears anyone finding out that they do, in fact, *love* their parents' music. The long-term social effects of friends discovering that one thinks 'Bing Crosby could really swing' or that 'some of Daniel O' Donnell's album tracks aren't that bad' have not yet been fully researched but are thought to be so devastating that very few people can even risk being diagnosed.

[orig. der.: *parens*, parent; *musica*, music; *exsul*, outcast]

◄o►

parensophobia
fear of being a parent

Most people do not know this phobia exists until it is upon them. It can sometimes strike as late as a year after the birth of their 'little bundle' (**parensophobes** often subconsciously use euphemisms to disguise their fear). Then suddenly, VOOM, it's there. Common thoughts include: Hang on a minute, I'm not mature enough to do right by this little one; I'm not sensible enough to keep them out of trouble; I'm not a GROWN UP!

Like most illnesses, women are far better than men at coping with it. Women think 'Weird' for just a few seconds then forget it. For men, it can often be mistaken for their mid-life crisis; indeed, it sometimes *is* their mid-life crisis. A classic male **parensophobe** will usually try to take his baby everywhere with him, in its rocker: to the gym, shops, pub, etc. (cinemas can be tricky). Doctors do not know what cures **parensophobia**. All they know is that something happens: one day it's gone, and the **parensophobic** male is suddenly gripped by a genuine desire to test spellings and research Ofsted reports.

[orig. der.: *parens*, parent]

◄○►

parvocoquophobia
fear of eating at motorway services

This translates loosely as 'fear of the small chef' and comes from the Roman belief that diminutive cooks must somehow be bad (in that a cook should love his food and therefore be fat – if a cook is small, what is wrong with his own food?) Nowadays it has come to mean fear of eating at motorway services – those meals you are forced into considering and, in emergencies, eating when on a long journey. Symptoms are often rage – at the inflated premium added for the privilege of deep-frying your food – followed by extreme poverty. Occasionally a dawning realisation follows concerning the equivalent amount of food one could have bought for the same price in, for example, a) a supermarket, or b) a Third World country. Some sufferers become irascible when discussing the practice of charging for a sachet of pepper. Spare a thought for the sad *parvoco-quophobia pictura* sufferers: these have a genetic disorder of the eyes which prevents them from understanding the relationship between the photographs of the food in the laminated menu and the food which eventually arrives on their plate.

[orig. der.: *parvus*, small; *coqua*, cook]

◄○►

perdetophobia
fear of having not saved one's work

If you are lucky, the fear of having not saved your work on a computer is a fleeting twinge of panic, possibly a frantic moment of key-pressing, followed by a gushing, euphoric wave of relief that the document on which you spent the last two hours is alive and well. You can congratulate yourself on the fact that, although you had no autosave enabled (the equivalent of Evil Knievel doing jumps without tyres on his bike), once again you were saved by those beautiful words, 'recovered document'. For the **perdetophobe**, however, life does not seem to allow for quite such a happy ending. The **perdetophobe** lives in fear of not just his email archive going down the Superhighway Swanee, but his entire life's *magnum opus* (that book he's been working on for the past few years, the one that's going to make him a million). For a **perdetophobe**, the worst eight words in the world come from an IT engineer: 'Best turn it off and on again, squire.'

[orig. der.: *perdere*, to lose; *totus*, everything]

◂◦▸

perdituphobia
fear of getting caught

Not connected to **perdetophobia** (q.v.) in any way, **perdituphobia** is one of the so called friendly fears. A huge number of law-abiding citizens are thought to be **perdituphobes**, saved from a life –

or at least a moment – of crime simply by the fear of getting caught. The most they are probably prepared to risk in life is popping a 'pick 'n' mix' in their mouth before they get to the till. If they were ever tempted to throw caution to the wind, they would immediately dive after it to try and get it back. Ironically, **perdituphobia** can occasionally increase crime levels, too, as sufferers commit another crime to avoid being caught for the first, and so on. Classic **perdituphobes** include you, me, Nick Leeson and Father Christmas.

[orig. der.: *perditus*, ruined]

◄○►

perecibuphobia
fear of ordering from foreign menus

It used to be 'little islanders' who made up the bulk of **perecibuphobes**. They would sit in their Spanish resort, ordering a full English – enunciated very slowly – from their favourite restaurant, a notable Spanish eatery called Terry's Authentic English Café. Back home, they were the ones who managed to find the omelette and chips on the Indian take-away menu. Now, though, a new breed of **perecibuphobes** is emerging – one which simply can't understand the complete tosh written on the menus of some of our cities' finest upper-class restaurants. Sometimes, when a translation is provided, they cannot even understand it in English: 'Ghislaine of sweetbread on a eucalyptus sybarite, served with a starfruit chad' – I'm sorry? The explanation from the clichéd maitre d' provides no help, either. Most tend to bluff by asking for 'the fish' and just hoping there's one there, or sycophantically requesting a recommendation. Others have been known to nip to the gents' and Google words from the menu on their BlackBerry.

[orig. der.: *peregrinus*, foreign; *cibus*, fodder]

—◦—

perelinguaphobia
fear of speaking a foreign language

Whether one is on an Autobahn, autostrada or *route nationale*, it is impossible to escape the English abroad. At most roadside stops, one-invariably vies for service with a hairy-arsed bunch of Tommy chavsters, all loudly declaiming, 'Two full breakfasts, mate, both with fried bread.' Admittedly these folk show no signs of using a foreign language, yet they are not, strictly speaking,

perelinguaphobes. A real **perelinguaphobe** always *wants* to use a foreign language, it's just that they fear doing so. Often this means they migrate to the rear of a group, pushing forward someone who seems to remember more of, say, their school French than they themselves do. Other options for the **perelinguaphobe** include mastering only the verbal trimmings of a language, so to speak, but with a heavy accent. In French, for example, this would mean procrastinating with 'mmmm . . . errrr . . . phhhh . . . (shrug of shoulders) . . . ohhhh . . . mmm . . . *Bof!*' And that's when someone has just said 'bonjour.' Another option is the ingenious '*Point It*' book, which contains pictures of everything you might ever need on holiday; you take it with you wherever you go and point to it whenever you're in trouble. Now and again, a remembered word will pop into the head, of even the most chronic **perelinguaphobe**, like a long-lost friend turning up out of the blue, sending them into paroxysms of delight because they remembered the Spanish word for hubcap.*

[orig. der.: *peregrinus*, foreign; *lingua*, tongue]

*It's *tapacubo*, by the way

—◦—

picaphobia
fear of seeing magpies

Stemming from a belief that magpies are somehow unlucky, **picaphobia** is originally a child's disease, thought to last no longer than the average schoolboy crush on Jenny Hanley. When, sadly, it does continue into old age, it can be debilitating. As can the crush on Jenny Hanley. Some sufferers concoct their own personal methods for dealing with each magpie they see – a **picaphobic** friend of mine has to pull her ears three times with both hands for each ill-starred bird. This can be tricky when driving a car. Symptoms of **picaphobia** include desperately racing through the words of the song to check if they have seen a bad number ('Five for silver . . . Fantastic . . . no worries'). Frequently, if a **picaphobe** sees one magpie – for sorrow – they might look away and then look back, to make it two, swearing that 'a mate of mine met a man in a pub once who knew Mick Robertson and he said it worked'.

[orig. der.: *pica*, magpie]

pluracanophobia
fear of watching something on the wrong channel

This has only recently been upgraded from a class C 'worry' to an actual phobia, having developed with the explosion of channels available on the nation's televisions. The **pluracanophobe** simply cannot keep up with this huge choice. They fear watching *ER* on the wrong side, for example, and thus seeing it out of order, thereby ruining the impact of what we used to call 'the last episode' (but which now goes by the rather grand name of the feature-length series finale). *ER* is a great case in point. Did they see it on digital, terrestrial or maybe even DVD? Was it Channel 4, E4, E4 + 1, More4, More4 + 1 or More-E4+1-take-away-the-first-number-you-thought-of? You see the **pluracanophobe**'s dilemma? The main problem programmes are ones like *ER*, *The Sopranos* and, of course, *Little Britain*. In the latter case, even the channel schedulers don't know where they are. Special mention should be made of *pluracanophobia amici*, or the so-called *Friends* phobia. This is when any confusion over which episode a sufferer has or hasn't seen has long been forgotten. When they happen to catch a previously unseen episode of the programme, then, it acts as a kind of visual Mogadon, bringing a sad, vacant smile to the sufferer's dribbling face, until nurse wheels them back to their room.

[orig. der.: *plurimus*, most; *canalis*, channel]

⬅◇➤

poculophobia
fear of 'coffee to go' cups

Poculophobia translates, more or less, as fear of cups, which seems a little indiscriminate considering sufferers fear only a tiny minority of the species, namely the take-away cup. 'To drink from the flimsy cup', as **poculophobes** term it, is to risk all manner of personal tragedy. The original form of the disease came about after the advent of polystyrene cups, those brittle yet bendy pieces of nonsense which crumble if you look at them, filling your brew with a magical collage of tiny specks of white cack. *Poculophobia nova* seems to affect mainly the *Friends* generation, who find that the modern take-away cup is a little too thin, occasionally resulting in third degree burns. This has been more or less stamped out by the corrugated card cup-holder. Pity, though, the small but sad handful of people afflicted with *poculophobia foramenia*. These people fear the hole at the top of the cup, particularly the DIY pin-back hole, which is often bordered with a self-evident warning embossed into the plastic (something like 'Contents may act as napalm' or what have you). They have become more than a little paranoid, managing to convince themselves that the coffee will take any route out of the cup except the one via the DIY opening. They are easily spotted by the latte up their nose.

[orig. der.: *poculum*, cup]

postophobia
fear of being late

It is often hard to tell a **seruphobe** (q.v.) and a **postophobe** apart. Strictly, a **postophobe** fears being late – not simply oversleeping. As a result, where you and I might allow ourselves, say, ten minutes' leeway in our journey times, **postophobes** will allow an hour. Or maybe two. Hell, why not go the day before and take a sleeping bag? In truth, it is not unknown for a **postophobe** to arrive at a job interview some three hours early, thus allowing themselves plenty of time to nip to Starbucks to get a coffee, do some last-minute interview thinking, read *Anna Karenina*, that sort of thing. (In dealing with **postophobes**, many doctors will eventually work out by how long the patient is always early for their sessions and so decide the precise nature of the treatment required. Eventually, they also manage to allow for early arrival and thus set accurate appointment times.) Occasionally, being a **postophobe** has been known to pay dividends: checking into an easyJet flight for example. Usually, though, it is a millstone round the necks of sufferers and their families, as anyone who has started queuing for the January sales in October will tell you.

[orig. der.: *post*, afterwards]

◄o►

praelocuphobia
fear of a certain drawer

Although by definition afraid of a certain drawer, a **praelocuphobe** in actual fact fears the contents of the drawer and their complete inability to be master of those contents. In terms of contents, we're talking unused key rings, several (mini) rolls of sticky tape, new *and* used batteries mixed together so that they have no idea which are any use – all these things add up to a profound nightmare for the **praelocuphobe**. More than this, though, **praelocuphobes** fear that, if they open the drawer, they will be able to find too many things they don't need but cannot throw out; or they will discover many things they never knew they had – but *still* won't throw out. If a **praelocuphobe** fails to avoid this first step and proceeds to 'enter the labyrinth' (open the drawer, in our language), they will at that point enter a world similar to that of the puzzle section of *The Krypton Factor*. They will open the drawer, take things out . . . then never quite manage to get them back in again, regardless of the fact that Gordon Burns is *not* stood there, shouting 'only thirty seconds left'. *Praelocuphobia mane* sufferers fear that something will become wedged in the drawer and so prevent them getting it open, and that they will have to stick a hand in to rescue the situation. In general, **praelocuphobia** is known not to afflict children. Children greet the drawer's useless objects with individual gasps of discovery, as if they were Columbus stumbling upon the Americas.

[orig. der.: *praecipuus*, special; *locus*, place]

---

presummaphobia
fear of being told the result of a
sporting event

This is a seasonal disorder which causes its sufferers to cross the road to avoid glancing in the window of a television shop. Other common symptoms include cupping the hands over the ears, and the chanting the mantra: 'La la la . . .

not listening . . . la la la . . .' True, **presumma-phobes** won't even turn on a radio or television if they are in Motson's Interlude (as therapists call the period which comes after the full-time whistle but before you've seen the game). A further, rarer strain is *presummaphobia aspecta*, the fear that, when the newscaster speaks those ten immortal words, 'Anyone not wishing to know the result, look away now,' one will somehow be compelled, like Lot's wife, to look over one's shoulder and clock it. This moment of looking away, incidentally, is known by **presummaphobes**, as the Golden Silence. When they 'hear' this silence, they pretty much know they have done it. They then sit down, lager in right hand, remote in left, put on their recording and realise they have recorded *Open University*.

[orig. der.: *praecipuus*, special; *summa*, summary]

-◦-

primaforaphobia
fear of being the first to leave work

The decline of the trade union movement is thought to be one of the contributing factors in the threefold increase of **primaforaphobia** over the last thirty years. Early diagnosis is considered important but is also very difficult, as most sufferers refuse to take time off to seek treatment. Therapists say the first sign of **primaforaphobia** is often the 'Trojan email', a missive sent as early as possible in the morning. Even though its subject line may read, 'Those figures from Hong Kong you wanted', the real point of any Trojan email is to advertise that you were in work at the crack of dawn. Thus, the **primaforaphobe** is implicitly saying, let me walk out of the office at a reasonable hour without shouting, 'Oh, half-day?' The main cause of **primaforaphobia** is the thought of redundancy; ironic, really, because redundancy is also the only known cure.

[orig. der.: *primus*, first; *foras*, outside]

––◦––

priormotaphobia
fear of the making the first move

A universal fear from which even the most confident amongst us have suffered at some time, over the years. The thrill of the chase, the first furtive brushing of the knee, the fake hitting that simply screams of a desire for contact – gorgeous moments to many but the equivalent of scraping your nails down a blackboard to the **priormotaphobe**. Moments like these mean that sufferers, who desperately want to woo like Rock Hudson in a Doris Day movie, end up wooing like Hugh Grant in that scene from *Four Weddings and a Funeral*. Many end up as **virgophobes** (q.v.).

[orig. der.: *prior*, first; *motus*, movement]

—◁◦▷—

prooemiophobia
fear of foreplay

Is this a fear? For some, the answer seems to be a firm yes. Partners of **prooemiophobes** often have perfectly stunning sex but just long for 'a bit of build up', so to speak. It's like going to great restaurants, eating superb main courses, but never being allowed a starter. **Prooemiophobia** affects men, obviously, and principally those who don't see the point of the Pearl and Dean ads or the film preview trailers when they go to the cinema, preferring instead just to turn up in time for the main film. (Ironically, partners of **prooemiophobes** secretly long for the days when they would not only show ads and previews but

also a nice short before the main feature.*)
Interestingly, sufferers can laugh heartily at the
scene in Monty Python's 'The Meaning of Life'
in which John Cleese 'teaches' a live sex lesson
to his class, but are often secretly bemused by the
comments about 'getting the juices flowing'. Some
therapists have testified that they can also guffaw
at the joke about the Australian definition of foreplay being a shouted 'Brace yourself, Sheila', but,
when pressed, cannot say why it is funny.

* On a separate but connected issue, researchers also found
that women tend to stay and watch right to the end of the
film credits, whereas men rush off as soon as the music
starts.

[orig. der.: *prooemium*, prelude]

◄◦►

propriophobia
fear of your family

Translating as 'fear of your own', this is something with which most of us can learn to live and
come to terms. Some doctors think it starts in
middle childhood, and that a daughter's embar-
rassment with her father, for example, or a son's
disgust at being asked to 'play your grade 1 piece

for the vicar . . . go on, go on . . .' are all part of the early onset. Who knows? What is certain is that full-blown **propriophobia** can be very painful indeed. Mad aunts wearing plus fours whom you meet at rare extended family gatherings; relatives who slap your stomach and say, 'Get that weight off!'; cousins with more A levels and better toys: they are all part of the syndrome. It is a problem that gets worse with age. When young, you can slope off to kids' bedrooms and play with alien toys. Later, you don't get that option. At least not without raising suspicions. Therapists have called the problem the Viscosity Principle: as blood is thicker than water, you do not have the option of dealing with your family as you would if they were just another member of the general public who you will never meet again. You just can't say, 'Oh my word, you really do have the dress sense of Barbara Cartland in her "Oxfam" period, don't you?' The Viscosity Principle prevents it. So you become a closet **propriophobe**. You smile, politely, over cheesy nibbles, while inside your heart has fallen off its chair and nearly died laughing at Auntie Maureen's gift of a home-knitted pullover.

[orig. der.: *proprius*, one's own]

◄○►

proscriptiophobia
fear of commercial television

Have you ever noticed how, whenever you visit a home for the infirm or elderly, the television is always tuned to ITV? Why is that? Does it act like a sort of visual Mogadon? Doctors are divided over this fear, which translates literally as 'fear of the adverts'. Some refuse to prescribe anything for it, saying it is more a sign of common sense than a fear. Others, though, recognise the discomfort it causes sufferers and are happy to prescribe the standard cure (take four videos of *Dad's Army* a day). Doctors are confident that **proscriptiophobia** will be all but eradicated within a few years as younger generations are becoming accustomed to commercial television at a much earlier age. Adverts for loan consolidation and no-win-no-fee solicitors – bizarrely screened on daytime preschoolers' channels – are helping most kids kick **proscriptiophobia** as early as aged four. Indeed, careers officers have reported that Channel Scheduler has now replaced Train Driver as the number one job ambition.

[orig. der.: *proscriptio*, advertisement]

quasumegophobia
fear of asking directions

Another 'male only' fear. Sufferers adopt steely smiles to disguise inner panic. In extreme cases, they will chant the **quasumegophobe**'s motto, 'It's just round this next corner, don't worry', and then lock all car doors and windows. It should be said that **quasumegophobes** do not fear getting lost, as, nine times out of ten, they already *are* lost – something they just will not accept (and you can't fear something that you don't think exists). For a **quasumegophobe**, maps are like fairies: they simply don't believe in them. As children, they eschewed dressing up as doctors and nurses, leaving friends bemused by disguising themselves as Scott of the Antarctic or Marco Polo. Occasionally, they would invite pals round to watch and re-watch *Monte Carlo or Bust*. Ironically, they are keen adopters of SatNav technology, often asking for it to be delivered in plain brown envelopes. Ultimately, **quasumego-phobes** fear being proven wrong, particularly amongst friends. It's not simply about routes. It's an innate refusal to believe John Donne's dictum that 'no man is an island'. In fact, come to mention it, they're fairly sure they know the *way* to that island . . . 'It's just round the next corner, don't worry.'

[orig. der.: *qua*, where; *sum*, am; *ego*, I]

—◦—

quisquiliaphobia
fear of junk mail

Often misdiagnosed as **versuphobia** (q.v.) **quisquiliaphobia** becomes ever more common with each additional felled tree. Most **quisquiliaphobes** fear *every* piece of junk mail, from local flyer to free newspaper (yes, considered junk mail in this context). Specific strains include *quisquiliaphobia victoria*, the fear of junk mail that tells you you have won something, complete with labyrinthine details on how to scratch off sections, affix offer C to card K and use envelope marked 'Yes, I'd like to claim my own, free, sovereign country'. *Quisquiliaphobia celata* is the particular fear of stuff that falls out of your Sunday paper on the way back from the newsagent. More recently, we have seen the increase of *quisquiliaphobia spamia* – the fear of junk emails – and *quisquiliaphobia salutatoria* – the fear of being rung by someone from a call centre in Bangalore and asked if you have considered switching utility suppliers).

[orig. der.: *quisquiliae*, rubbish; *victor*, winner; *celata*, secrets; *salutatio*, greeting]

---

respraeterphobia
fear of missing something

This usually starts in childhood and can be difficult to shake off, particularly for middle children. It is not dissimilar, at least in effect, to **antefamaphobia** (q.v.) and, in fact, some doctors have difficulty telling them apart. Symptoms start with a vocal tick in which the sufferer is heard to say, constantly, 'What? . . . What? What is it?' This is often replaced by deep paranoia and even the odd **antefamaphobic** attack. **Respraeterphobes** are thought to make up around 70 per cent of people who ring into radio competitions (many have not even heard the question, but simply rang when they heard a number being read out). **Respraeterphobes** will take free samples of anything given out by promotional models, regardless of the content. Free piece of cheese? Yes please. Free oversized plastic thimble of wine?

Go on then. Free locust on a stick? Yes, and could I take one for my friend. **Respraeterphobes** will wait at the stage door of a theatre when they haven't even been to see the show. In fact, they will join any queue or gathering crowd, even though they may not know the reason it is gathering. Sometimes easily confused with the medical condition 'densusia': being thick.

[orig. der.: *res*, something; *praetor*, beyond]

━◦━

rimpavophobia
fear of standing on the cracks in the pavement

Although not on a par with, say, vertigo, this fear is still very serious to its sufferers. Who are, generally, between the ages of three and seven. They do not fear the contact of *pied à terre*, so to speak; they fear all the things that go with it. Some are taught that 'stand on the cracks in the pavement and the bogeyman will come from his subterranean cave and take you back'. Or that they will 'fall in, and be swept underground'. Or that they will 'inadvertently trigger the opening of a time-port into another continuum', wherein they will spend 'giga-years, before returning to earth as a marker pen' (this last lot tend to be offspring of IT workers who watch *Buffy*). Symptoms include jerky, quixotic movement from a to b, the gripping of an adult's hand until it is white, and complete inertia when confronted by a mosaic floor.

[orig. der.: *rima*, crack; *pavimentum*, pavement]

---

rotathecaphobia
fear of trolley suitcases

Rotathecaphobes generally split into two groups, because of the two distinct types of trolley suit-cases they fear. *Rotathecaphobia prima* affects the far greater number, everyday people like you and me, who might have been tipped over the edge by 'tourist tractors' (a tourist tractor is any suitcase, on wheels, which has the seemingly sudden capacity to extend the user's rear personal space by a small, but deadly, metre). Most *r.p.* sufferers cite railway stations, airports and busy streets as the places where they first displayed symptoms. *Rotathecaphobia seconda* sufferers are more . . . shall we say, alternative. They fear the pathetically tiny corporate trolley cases, beloved of short-sleeved middle managers, reps and international hitmen. Although smaller than the traditional version – some say this makes them harder to avoid – their allied corporate culture makes the fear of them all the more virulent. Some doctors think both conditions can be treated, alongside *clamsaccophobia oscillaia* – fear of swinging backpacks – but insufficient supporting research exists. Symptoms of *r.s.* and *r.p.* include bruised toes, inability to proceed forwards and a propensity to violence.

[orig. der.: *rota*, wheel; *theca*, case]

◄○►

rufophobia
fear of ginger-haired people

Totally irrational – yet, for some, totally understandable – **rufophobia** divides doctors in the same way that Anne Robinson's comments on the Welsh did. **Rufophobia**: totally unfounded, say some; agreed, say others. Having said that, however, ginger people do smell of wee and cheat at cards, don't they? Common strains include *rufophobia C.E.*, which causes sufferers to fear seeing repeats of *TFI Friday*; *rufophobia A.V.*, where they can't stand the music of the famous redhead Vivaldi; and *rufophobia M.H.*, where any Simply Red track can lead to violent fits. It is from the early diagnoses of **rufophobia** that we are thought to have gained the phrase 'to see red'.

[orig. der.: *rufus*, red-haired]

---

rusmusophobia
fear of country music

Although it is not strictly classed as such, many consider this to be one of the 'friendly fears'. The jazz drummer Buddy Rich did much to break the taboo on this cruel affliction on his deathbed, when he allegedly was asked by a nurse if anything was bothering him. 'Country music' was his reply, and so began a refreshing period of openness about 'the illness that dare not speak its name unless accompanied by a slide guitar'. Therapists tend to work on helping sufferers come to terms with the Three Fs they fear: fashion (doctors work with the patient to introduce checked shirts, checked trousers, checked swimming trunks, etc.); feet (slowing encouraging wayward limbs to point and line dance); and feelings (which can soon be made to focus on epic melancholy, epic love, or epic melancholic love). From being fans of anything from thrash metal to Ambrosian chant, patients are guided (assisted listening, it is called) through apparently non-ironic songs about menfolk whose wives left them in favour of anything from another man to an emperor penguin. **Ex-rusmusophobes** tend to listen to such songs before going home and beating up their own. Wives, that is, not emperor penguins.

[orig. der.: *rusticus*, country; *musicus*, music]

---

saltaphobia
fear of dancing

Many people cannot understand **saltaphobes**. Fear of dancing? Dancing is just dancing, right? Why should anyone *fear* dancing? Well, for a **saltaphobe**, dancing is up there with eating your internal organs. First of all, there's the dance floor, which is very often surrounded by a gallery on which people sit and watch. Then, there's the fact that it is communal. Yes, sufferers would gladly go into a private booth and thrash their arms about *on their own* but . . . *with everyone else*? Finally, of course, there is the fact that they are the rhythmic version of tone-deaf. Whoever it was who said, 'All God's chillun' got rhythm', well, he never saw the St Michael's College disco in Leeds in the late seventies. **Saltaphobes** are often **saltaphobes** *with good reason*. They long to get up and impress à la John Travolta in *Saturday Night Fever*, but whenever they do overcome their fears for just a moment, friends begin to look distressed and shout 'What were you thinking of?' before calling for a nurse. Thankfully, though, **saltaphobia** is now totally cured in some social groups – middle-aged dads who iron their jeans, for example. I say *thankfully* . . .

[orig. der.: *saltare*, to dance]

sapophobia
fear of watching soaps

Originally just a specific form of **deditophobia** (q.v.), this was only reclassified as a grade one fear – rather than just a strain – in 1992, largely due to the launch of the BBC's *Eldorado*. Up until this point, soaps were not considered *too* destructive. **Sapophobes** are unfortunate individuals. They say they don't *like* a certain soap, and yet they fear that, if they watch it, they will get hooked. Sadly, many **sapophobes** are in relationships and cite a partner as the catalyst for their addiction, particularly **bulliphobic** (q.v.) partners. Recently, doctors have been working on the non-addictive soap, and early developments were considered promising with the daytime launch of *Doctors*.

[orig. der.: *sapo*, soap]

—◦—

scalapellophobia
fear of see-through stairs

When the new flagship Apple building opened in London's Regent Street, just a couple of years ago, a fair few sex-starved, squinting geeks queued up for days to be the first in. Pity, then, the *Star Trek*-loving **scalapellophobe** who rushed in that first Saturday morning, desperate to get to the first floor: Apple had spent the equivalent of the national debt of Tonga on a breathtaking, central *glass* stairway. To the **scalapellophobe**, the construction of such a stairway is not a million miles away from what Mengele was doing with his experiments in the war. **Scalapellophobia** is more common and, in fact, less modern, than one might think. It was first identified in 1851 at the Crystal Palace exhibition, when the Prince of Wales was forced to have a sitdown with a cup of tea and a bun on his way up to the first floor. A mini-epidemic was reported in 1934 when several of Busby Berkely's dancers went down with it at once. A rarer strain is *scalapellophobia pons*, which affects pedestrians who fear crossing bridges with gaps in them. It makes traversing very difficult and playing Pooh-sticks nigh on impossible.

[orig. der.: *scalae*, stairs; *pellucidus*, transparent; *pons*, bridge]

scalaphobia
fear of escalators

Scalaphobia is one word for what is, in fact, many fears. In its original form, it is fear of the escalator itself. What causes it? Possibly new technology, possibly the continual motion; doctors don't really know. Soon, though, **scalaphobia** came to mean fear of the escalator *killing you*. This is thought to stem from an urban myth in which somebody is said to have trapped their shoelace. When the escalator reached the bottom, they are said to have been dragged into the machine and to a grisly death akin to being put through a giant shredder. Another story has the person actually falling into a weakened step and becoming trapped up to their waist in the escalator, to be dissected at the top. It should be stressed that these are urban myths. Pleasant. Elsewhere, *scalaphobia aequia* is becoming more common. This is a fear of the long, horizontal escalators that convey travellers to and from flight gates. Frequent flyers try to overcome this phobia by walking hurriedly alongside, with a trolley, shouting dates and times into their Bluetooth earpiece, desperate to prove that they can beat the escalator. Other rare but virulent strains include *scalaphobia taberna* – this occurs when travelling over a number of floors and thus using a number of escalators. *S.t.* is, in actual fact, the fear of seeing something you hadn't come in for but now want to buy, in a department store, before being able to find the next escalator in the series. Also recognised is *scalaphobia immota*, an irrational fear of using an escalator that has been turned off or has broken down. Failure to acknowledge *s.i.* can result in the strange sensation whereby one treats the first few steps on a motionless escalator as if it were working, only to come to an ungainly, clumping halt. Sufferers who find themselves, halfway up, using the escalator at the very moment it is actually switched off can be often be stranded there for hours.

[orig. der.: *scalae*, stairs; *aequus*, level; *taberna*, shop; *immotus*, motionless]

—◦—

sedsocophobia
fear of sitting next to the wrong person at a dinner party

Wrong, in this instance, can mean anything from torpor-inducingly dull to one fork short of a setting. If you are **sedsocophobic**, it almost invariably means that you have had a bad experience in the past. As a result, you get nervous while preparing to go out to visit friends. A chronic **sedsocophobe** will have thought about (even discussed) seating plans some days earlier. Often, though, as they are getting changed pre-excursion, they freeze by the wardrobe and remember vividly the man who was 'in aggregates' and talked for at least twenty-five minutes about shale. Therapists say some sufferers even take their own name-place cards to parties and are prepared to shuffle and rearrange, often leaving the hosts totally bemused. An offshoot strain, *sedsocophobia itinera*, occurs when a person fears who might sit next to them on a bus. This is a much more passive affliction, in that sufferers have no chance to alter their temporary destiny other than by standing up or getting off the bus. Sometimes the fear that can accrue – on the top deck, in just the time it takes someone who has just got on to walk from the top of the stairs to, thankfully, the seat behind them – can be life-threatening.

[orig. der.: *sedere*, to sit; *sociare*, to socialise; *iteneris*, journey]

◄◦►

semelophobia
fear of never seeing someone again

Semelophobia is a temporal fear, said to strike most on public transport, in art galleries and in supermarkets. Interestingly, it isn't the queasy feeling of fear that strikes first; it is a simple rush of desire. The sufferer, usually male, sees what Desmond Morris would call a potential mate and manages, instantaneously, to convince himself would be the one for him if only he were to a) meet her, b) be single and c) not be living in his own little cumulus named Cuckoo. Unknown to him, he has in this short time become a **semelophobe**: he fears this is a *once-only* meeting. In an age where impromptu, ritual mating dances are somewhat out of fashion, he is left with two choices. He can simply walk on and, no doubt, forget all about it. Or he can tread a fine line between the sweet, mad fool and Keith the local stalker by changing his plans, that moment, and pursuing her. Symptoms include shortness of breath, sweaty palms and red cheeks from being slapped. Famous **semelophobes** include James Blunt, the Impulse advert man and, sadly, Keith the local stalker.

[orig. der.: *semel*, once]

senecophobia
fear of growing old

They are wearing Bench jeans, but have ironed a hardy, sensible crease right down the middle of them. They have a Sigur Ros CD in their collection but don't know how to pronounce it. They are, almost certainly, **senecophobes**. Poor creatures. These two symptoms are tiny in relation to the main manifestation of the disease, which is the adoption of *lingua iuventa*, or youth speak. Hence many a therapist has recommended a course of Cliff Richard concerts to their patient, only to be told to 'get real, that's so not going to happen. Er, doctor.' Petrified at the prospect of taking up bowls or subscribing to *People's Friend*, **senecophobes** are possibly more of a problem for their children than themselves. The offspring are forced to become 'don't-carers', shunning their loved ones for their own good. Incidentally, nothing cheers up a **senecophobe** as much as that gorgeous moment when they realise that an old phrase they used to use has become hip again. Like 'hip', for example.

[orig. der.: *senecta*, old age]

sermophobia
fear that someone will talk to you

Many doctors think **sermophobia** and **umerser-mophobia** (q.v.) are related, but this is unproven. **Sermophobes** are very common. Most daily commuters are **sermophobes**. Despite the fact that they have been travelling from their leafy suburb with, more or less, the same bunch of familiar faces for the last twelve years, they fear talking to any of them – save for the friendly half-smile which is Commuter for a) Good morning, b) Sorry, did I hit you with my folding Brompton bike? and/or c) any other phrase at all, actually. Fortunately, thanks to the unwritten yet extensive Commuter Code, the feared situation will hardly ever occur. Many sufferers know this in their hearts but still fear those times when an older, non-commuter boards the train and engages them in what, in not too far off an age, would have passed for normal conversation. Not only are they forced to converse, they also know that their fellow commuters are hearing their agonies. 'Oh, I see: you're going to meet your son in London. How lovely,' they are compelled to reply. *Aaaaaagggghhhhhhhh*, the agony of it. How will they live it down? Next day, of course, they say nothing. But . . . are they saying nothing because they always say nothing? Or are they saying nothing because they are . . . well, *saying nothing*?

[orig. der.: *sermo*, conversation]

---

seruphobia
fear of oversleeping

Not to be confused with insomnia, although some-times the symptoms are similar – that is, waking up every hour, on the hour. Whereas the insom-niac's lack of sleep is physical, the seruphobe's is mental. He or she has something in-built that makes them wake up, to see if it is time to get up – a sort of body clock with a faulty alarm, something shared by abemoraphobes (q.v.). The sad thing for the **seruphobe** – from the Latin *sero* meaning too late – is that, most of the time, it isn't. Too late, that is. **Seruphobes** are usually easy to spot by their constant yawning, baggy eyes and detailed knowledge of News 24 presenters.

[orig. der.: *serus*, late]

socruphobia
fear of the mother-in-law

This is a cruel one. Many fears stake some claim, in some form, to be the fear that dare not speak its name (see **rusmusophobia, uxophobia** and **vilitasophobia**); this one comes closest. **Socruphobia** has to be borne and cannot be allowed to show itself in any way other than in jokes. In fact, when **socruphobes** get together in their self-help groups – or 'go for a pint', as they are forced to say – they often open the proceedings by reading a Les Dawson joke, in Latin. Some even have the jokes made into a group motto – notable the West Yorkshire Young Sons-in-Law Group, whose members are compelled to learn the oath, 'I must dash: the mother-in-law's lost her voice and I don't want to miss a minute of it.' The most common, tell-tale symptoms of **socruphobia** include late nights at work and a veritable campaign to be allowed to turn the spare room at home into an office. Interestingly, *the* mother-in-law is actually the correct usage: *my* or *your* should never be used.

[orig. der.: *socrus*, mother-in-law]

◄○►

solverophobia
fear of letting go

Most parents have suffered at least a twinge of this disease at some stage but only about 30–40 per cent will ever contract full-blown **solverophobia**. Symptoms range from the simple over-questioning of one's children to, in extreme cases, the attempted humiliation of their boy and girlfriends. Ways of achieving this humiliation vary from basic awkward questions ('So, I hear you've got GCSE woodwork, Conan – thinking of going into the City?') to ousting them during the slow dance at parties. Also common is **pre-solverophobia**, affecting parents of preschool children who fear that, come the time, they will not be able to let go. This long-term self-awareness does nothing to prevent **solverophobia** itself taking hold, strangely enough.

[orig. der.: *solvere*, to loosen]

—◦—

squalidophobia
fear of untidiness

If you have ever seen the classic movie *The Odd Couple*, you will recognise Felix Ungar as a **squalidophobe**. A more recent television example would be Monica from *Friends*. You probably know one of these people. Or, if you are one yourself, you probably haven't a clue what I'm talking about. Fear of untidiness? That's not a phobia, that's just common sense, isn't it? In fact, up until *Friends*, **squalidophobes** never really sought help. Doctors think the character of Monica brought the issue out into the open and possibly even broke the taboo on the practice of carrying around a spare Toilet Duck and Marigolds, 'just in case'. (For a complete history of **squalidophobia** in television and film, read Halliwell's *Another Fine Mess?*, Mundus and Mundus, 1993.) Most **squalidophobes** realise what they are when they go to college or university – in fact, any situation that forces them to cohabit with a number of different people. Police files show numerous cases of being called out to document a reported burglary, only to find that the complainant was **squalidophobic** and that 'a spoon had been left out on the surface, complete with a stain'.

[orig. der.: *squalidus*, filthy]

-◄○►-

stolidophobia
fear of starting a crossword in public

Most **stolidophobes** are train commuters, with cases being more prevalent on Oxford and Cambridge lines. For **stolidophobes**, who tend to have train buddies rather than friends, the decision to commence a crossword is brave. How far can they proceed before the crossword setter shows them exactly *why* he chose the name of some particularly vicious character in Greek mythology? **Stolidophobes** fear being able to complete only the easy, anagram clues and then having to decide what to do next. Bluff, and fill in blanks with names of First World War battles? What if someone asks 'how they arrived at Passchendaele' for 8 across? Especially as it's only six letters. **Stolidophobes** generally yawn, feign fatigue and mumble something about 'finishing it later'. Doctors recently identified two new 'superbug' strains: *stolidophobia innumer-*

abilis and *stolidophobia innumerabilis genus alter*. Both concern the irritant Sudoku. *S.i.* attacks the sufferer in much the same way, as its letter-based relation, differing only in that numbers are much easier to bluff – unless you find yourself sat next to Carol Vorderman on the train. *S.i.g.a.* – known colloquially as 'genius envy' – afflicts people in the vicinity of Sudoku players. Symptoms are, nevertheless, more virulent. They include a sensation of not being on the bandwagon and a whole host of feelings, ranging from mild irritation to a desire to throw passengers from the train. Too early for a cure.

[orig. der.: *stolidus*, stupid]

—◦—

subturrophobia
fear of getting an erection in public

Thought to be derived from the Latin *subito* (sudden) and *turris* (tower). Sufferers of this painfully debilitating disease comprise three distinct groups: beach **subturrophobes,** sleep **subturrophobes** and – most sizeably – school disco **subturrophobes.** As their names suggest, each group's individual differences stem mainly from geography – b.s. sufferers, for example, fear the stiffie on the beach, while s.d.s. sufferers fear the youthful pocket Mars bar during the slow dance at the end. The exception is the s.s. sufferer, who fears waking up on a train to find he has a lap lighthouse. For most, though, the fear is far worse than the eventual erection, particularly amongst those who also suffer from **exiturrophobia** (q.v.). Despite its modern categorisation, **subturrophobia** is thought to date from as far back as 1500 BC, when Hercules disgraced himself during the now lost 13th Labour, 'The Embarrassing Great Trouser Tent of Tassos' (see Ovids *Tales from the Crotch*).

[orig. der.: *subito*, sudden; *turris*, tower]

◄○►

supsuescaphobia
fear of Ikea

This may be a tiny fear in terms of actual numbers of sufferers, but it is awfully potent when it strikes. Cruelly, too, it affects the memory. **Supsuescaphobia** makes its sufferers forget they have the ailment, a process thought to be very similar to the way in which a mother will forget the pain of childbirth in time to think, 'Let's do it all again.' **Supsuescaphobes** only get an inkling that something is wrong with them when they have gone back to the store and are walking round the set route, with dwarf pencils and paper tape-measures, saying things like, 'Do you have any more of the Titvat shelves? Or the Plǿk wardrobes?' The full force of their phobia hits them when they have made it past the bargain basement section, though, and suddenly they see an M25 of queues, not one of them less than a hundred people long and with trolleys the size of forklift trucks, full of entire roomfuls of furniture. A **supsuescaphobe** will, at this point, most likely ditch his trolley and slope off to the Ikea café, to drown their sorrows in meatballs and sweet purple juice.

[orig. der.: *supellex*, furniture; *suescere*, to become accustomed to]

◄○►

tabernaphobia
fear of shopping

When Marks and Spencer introduced the 'man crèche' into their Oxford Street store in London, they were responding to the huge global increase in **tabernaphobia** over the last decade. The man crèche consisted of an easy-chair area, gentlemen's quarterlies and boys' toys. The people you found in the man creche would, almost certainly, have been **tabernaphobes**, most of them pushed over the edge by just one fitting-room session too many. Years of trailing round after their **magnafundaphobe** (q.v.) has left most **tabernaphobes** (many of them **illerogophobes**, q.v., too) unable even to savour the pleasures of shopping on their own. (A survey for the male-only shopping website, heBay.com, says 74 per cent of men now prefer to shop online, with a staggering 82 per cent of those giving the reason that 'a website isn't worried about the size of its arse'.) A chronic **tabernaphobe** is easy to spot, not just in a shop but in any situation. Pick up a random obect – anything, anything at all – place it on your head and ask if it suits you. A true, chronic **tabernaphobe** will simply tell you, 'Yes, it's perfect. Now can we go?'

[orig. der.: *taberna*, shop]

tinniphobia
fear of one's phone ringing on a train

Despite being still a modern condition, **tinni-phobia** is well on its way towards total eradication. It proliferated in the nineties, when mobiles gradually evolved from machines the size of a phone box to the nanotechnology we have today. (Some feel that the rush to miniaturise has gone too far, with people holding micro-phones as if they were posh cucumber sandwiches, between thumb and forefinger.) Back in the nineties there were, as the papers say, 'red faces all round' if your mobile went off and you were forced to talk on a machine in public. **Tinniphobes** would talk monosyllabically and at such a low volume that even over-attentive librarians would be pressed to hear them. Now, some six years 'PDJ' (post-Dom Joly), doctors say that barking your company's tedious yet commercially sensitive financial secrets raucously down your mobile while all around you wince has all but replaced Travel Scrabble or rereading discarded newspapers as the nation's favourite train-journey pastime. (See **frigensophobia**, q.v.)

[orig. der.: *tinnire*, to ring]

—◦—

transpilophobia
fear of giving birth

The fact that you have almost certainly never heard of this as an actual phobia is not surprising, as the whole giving-birth thing is, at best, shrouded in secrecy and, at worst, a huge conspiracy theory to protect the propagation of the human race. That is, if women were told what it is really like to give birth, they simply wouldn't do it. **Transpilophobia** derives its name from a combination of the Latin words for 'to pass' and 'a football'. It can kick in at any time during the nine months between the possibly *great* actual few moments of conception and the almost certainly *awful* potential couple of days of birth. Grassy-knoll types will realise that words like (a) morning sickness and (b) nesting are mere covers, intended to put you off the true experiences of, respectively, (a) vomiting for a full four-month stretch and (b) going so potty that you keep arranging and rearranging the furniture like Lady Macbeth. Often, the **transpilophobe** feels they should avoid all this – until they are suddenly 'cured' by a mere smile from a toddler in a café. Then, there's nothing they can do about it. As Sven would say, you've just got to pass the ball.

[orig. der.: *transitus*, passage; *pila*, football]

◄o►

tympanophobia
fear of born-again Christians

This controlling fear takes its name from the Latin word for tambourine, *tympanum*, the favoured instrument of the BAC, and it can strike at any time. Often referred to therapists because of their word-for-word knowledge of *The Life of Brian*, **tympanophobes** can find their some-times brilliant logic no match for the sheer self-confidence of the BAC. A true **tympanophobe** would do well to steer away from signs for the Alpha Course and should not be allowed to hear even the introduction to Graham Kendrick's 'Shine, Jesus, Shine'.

[orig. der.: *tympanum*, tambourine]

◄o►

umersermophobia
fear of taxi drivers' conversation

For an **umersermophobe**, the perfect journey by cab is in absolute silence. They fear many things about talking to a cab driver but, principally, the tone of the conversation is top of the list. An **umersermophobe** can never imagine themselves emitting the phrase, 'Well . . . no actually, I *don't* think hanging's too good for them,' and therefore would rather not start talking. They may also worry about asking, 'So, have you been on long?' knowing that, if they are being honest, they have said this on 99 per cent of all taxi trips they've ever taken. And, if they are being even more honest, they don't care. Sufferers know that the conversation is going nowhere; it is in a vacuum. They would prefer simply to stare out of the window, adjust their seatbelt or, at a pinch, have another go at working out the relationship between the changing of the meter and the speed of the cab. Some **umersermophobes** fear conversation because, inexplicably, they feel compelled to share too much information. ('Why did I just tell him what I paid for my house and that my mother-in-law doesn't like *The West Wing*?)

Doctors have wondered whether the worry over how much to tip is connected, but so far this is unproven. (Incidentally – and I realise that this is sharing too much – the author is a chronic **umersermophobe**. Having said that, as far as he knows, he is alone in spending his time during cab journeys trying to picture the cab driver at home, insisting on putting his chair in front of his wife's and talking backwards at her, over his shoulder).

[orig. der.: *umerus*, shoulder; *sermo*, conversation]

◄○►

unicurrophobia
fear of special edition cars

Most of us can still suffer an attack of **unicurrophobia** on any long journey, simply by catching sight of a garish, multicolour trim and a stuck-on transfer name which seems to be ill-matched to the car sporting it: the Lada 101 '*Rio Di Janeiro*', for example, or the Volkswagen Bora '*Calypso*'. Although it is still very common, modern medicine has made massive strides towards eradicating this fear. It is now virtually wiped out amongst under-25 females and secretaries, for example. Other demographics amongst which fear of special edition cars is almost unknown include the 17–17.1-year-old, new-driver group; that is, those sad, bespectacled young girls and boys who get their picture taken in the local paper for passing their driving test at the age of seventeen and one day. In the background, take a look. See? There they are, tearing up their L-plates . . . in front of their Skoda Octavia '*Las Vegas*' special edition, with special gold trim.

[orig. der.: *unicus*, unique; *currus*, car]

—<o>—

uxorphobia
fear of one's wife

The author will gladly admit to many of the phobias in this book, but **uxorphobia** is not one of them. True, his wife told him to say that, but nevertheless . . . It is important to differentiate here, too. There are people who refer to their wife as 'her to be obeyed' or 'the boss'. These people tend not to be **uxorphobes**;

an **uxorphobe** would never actually dare speak in this way. On the contrary; **uxorphobia** is often known as the fear that dare not speak its name within earshot. **Uxorphobes** tend not to socialise with their wives. Then again, they don't socialise solo, either. In truth, they tend not to socialise at all, favouring a quasi-depressive state of inertia, known medically as *uxorphobia subpollexia*, from the Latin *pollex*, meaning thumb.

[orig. der.: *uxor*, wife]

◄○►

valephobia
fear of hospitals

The full, kennel name for this phobia is actually **valetudinariophobia**, but most doctors shorten it to the above. True **valephobes** won't even watch *Casualty*, never mind visit friends in hospital. They fear the look, the smell, the people in white coats; most of all, however, they fear that they might, somehow, never leave. In its male form, valephobia is often diagnosed when a patient lets slip that a nurse's outfit 'doesn't do anything for me.' **Valephobes** feel that being in a hospital will somehow bring them closer to their own end. Of course, courtesy of MRSA, they've bloody well been proven right, haven't they? Marvellous.

[orig. der.: *valetudinarium*, hospital]

―◦―

vaporphobia
fear of having left something on

Once, this was considered to be simply a 'seasonal disorder', hence its name derives from having left the gas on, as it was thought to afflict mainly holiday makers. Some doctors dismissed it as a mere 'inkling', refusing to treat people until the instances of their compulsion to stop the car and return home had reached double figures. It is now widely accepted that this seemingly minor phobia is far more prevalent than originally believed, and there is ongoing research to suggest that its remit should now be widened to include fear of having left the tap or the television on, and, more recently, the mobile uncharged. Sufferers say the malaise seems to strike most often while they are in meetings, and that symptoms include a sudden staring into space, a creeping feeling of butterflies in the stomach and a growing suspicion, amongst those around them, that they have joined a cult.

[orig. der.: *vapor*, gas]

vencelerphobia
fear of coming too soon

This male disorder affects not only the sex patterns but also the sleep patterns, with many sufferers complaining of the same, recurrent nightmare – namely playing as a striker for their favourite football team, but constantly shooting before they even get inside the other team's half. Sex therapist Gunther Wood says this dream is shared by a staggering 82 per cent of **vencelerphobes** (see his book *He Shoots, He Scores*, Tower Press, 2000). **Vencelerphobes** tend to try the 'deterrent notions' methods, to take their minds off their fears, most often conjuring up thoughts of baseball players or the inner workings of a Ford Capri automatic. It's a fine line to tread, of course, as it can have the undesired effect of deflating passion completely. Sufferers are easily identified by their heavier than normal sigh and the year-round glower – of their partners, that is.

[orig. der.: *venire*, to come; *celer*, quick]

—◦—

vendomophobia
fear of estate agents

In one of the first drafts of *Faust*, Goethe wrote a scene which was later removed by the censor, in which Faust seeks to sell his soul to the Devil via a 'soul agent', only to discover, when the latter turns up with horns and trident, that agent and Devil are one and the same. (The scene sees the agent describing Faust's soul as 'bijou yet well-appointed, with one loving owner, benefitting from a pleasant aspect'.) Today, for most **vendomophobes**, estate agents are just a little too much like young Tory hopefuls, minus the rosette. The whole **vendomophobia** syndrome is said to start as mere resentment, usually at giving away a sizeable percentage of the price of the house to unctuous game-show hosts who appear to do nothing more than ring you, if you're lucky, to say someone's on their way over. This can grow into a bona fide fear, the longer the house is on the market. Although, around 80 per cent of **vendomophobes** fear only the agent, some fear the estate agent's premises and/or their 'globilingua' – the actual medical term for talking bollocks. A tiny 1 per cent are even *vendomophobia excipens* sufferers, who fear the clusters of estate agents' offices which spring up in 'much sought-after' areas that have 'kept their price'. They dread driving through a village that boasts no village pub, no post office, no food shop even, yet somehow manages to maintain five estate agents on its tiny high street.

[orig. der.: *venditor*, seller; *domus*, house; *globi*, balls; *lingua*, language; *excipio*, exempt]

ventignophobia
fear of having farted out loud while listening to music on headphones

From the same family of phobias as **fortavoco-phobia** (q.v.), this socially disastrous complaint – like many little-known phobias – often strikes the sufferer whilst they are travelling. Symptoms include paranoia about frequent furtive glances from fellow passengers and unexplained feelings of guilt. Psychologists also have a saying: 'By all means cure the **ventignophobe**, but open a window first.' (See also **malventophobia**, q.v.)

[orig. der.: *ventus*, wind; *ignarus*, ignorant of]

◄◦►

verbaphobia
fear of text messaging

Verbaphobia is more than just 'a branch of techno-phobia', as some cynics have suggested. **Verba-phobes** can find themselves sucked into the disease via a Radio 4-induced distaste of all things to do with modern life. They might have started by merely 'disliking' the fact that their niece texts while at the dinner table, her endlessly darting thumb giving her the appearance of a hitchhiker with Tourette's. Now they find themselves in situations where texting would be fairly useful, but nevertheless they fear the entire process. Their friends have started doing it – albeit with the caveat that they will always text in full sentences, thus taking just a little longer than if they were to whittle the words out of pieces of driftwood using a penknife. (They text in full sentences because they once read a piece in the paper that appalled them, about the *Complete Works of Shakespeare* written in text, which had Richard III coming out as NW IS TH WNTA OF R DSCNTNT' and left 'MCBTH' sounding like a Happy Meal.) **Verbaphobes** themselves, though, simply cannot do it. Were they, say, to be stranded on top of Helvellyn, with a mobile phone minus its mouthpiece and only a text message standing between them and hypothermia, they still could not do it. Besides, even if they did, there's always the chance that their text could reach a fellow **verbophobe**, at the rescue centre, who could react badly: 'What's this . . . ? "HLP HLP, TRPD UP HLVLN. FRZNG CLD." Oh, I'm sorry, but that's not proper English. Sod 'em.'

[orig. der.: *verbum*, word]

versurphobia
fear of bills

Even the most inoffensive brown envelope can be enough to make the **versurphobe** nauseous and reach for the shredder. As the mantra goes, 'manilla + window + franking = rather high blood-pressure ranking'. In fact, violent reaction to the post provided the catalyst for one of the first decisive acts of the fledgling Scottish Parliament, i. e. the promise to postmen to introduce a compulsory Versurphile List – a comprehensive roll call of names and addresses – in order to allow mail to be delivered in safety ('Don't Shoot the Messenger' intiative, 2003). Other measures due to be tabled include compulsory emailing of statements and US-style 'throwing bills', enabling the postman to deliver from the gate. This fear is set to increase threefold in the next ten years, as a) credit becomes more and more available, b) debt continues to rise and c) banks become even bigger bastards.

[orig. der.: *versura*, borrowings]

◄o►

vertafundephobia
fear of jumping from a height for no apparent reason

Time has blurred the true meaning of this word which originally would have meant 'top to bottom' disease. It describes the symptoms – often felt only momentarily – that occur when a sufferer is confronted with the view from the top of a tall building or cliff and thinks, although there is no reason for them to do so, 'What if I just jumped off the edge?' As a result it is a member of the so-called *sedcur* family of diseases which, in most cases at least, elicit the response, 'But why would I?' Symptoms usually dissipate within seconds, although when they don't the result can be unpleasant (ref. the career of Eddie 'the Eagle' Edwards). First recorded by Pliny the Elder: 'Thursday: walked to roof of Pantheon. Got me an attack of the **vertafundaphobes** [*sic*]. Lasted merely seconds but still needed to change toga.' (From Pliny's *Historia naturalis*, 77 AD.)

[orig. der.: *vertex*, summit; *fundus*, bottom; *sed*, but; *cur*, why]

◄○►

viatorphobia
fear of tourists

Never take a **viatorphobe** to a fashion parade.
Not a very useful tip, I know, but one which
can only do good, nevertheless. To a **viatorphobe**,
the hollow whirr and motorised click of many
a modern camera reminds them of their fear.
They are instantly back in a large, bustling city,
and someone has just stopped dead in front of
them, to take a picture. **Viatorphobes** cannot
understand how people can walk so slowly.
Ironically, sufferers of a separate strain, *viator-
phobia duxia*, don't even fear tourists; they fear
the most annoying person of all: the teamleader
or guide. A V.d. sufferer can be rendered speechless if the teamleader, walking out in front, waves
their rolled-up newspaper or brolly. For straight-
forward **viatorphobes**, the babble of a foreign
language can act as a partial comfort, like the
calm lapping of a water feature. However, most
viatorphobes say that when confronted by an
English-speaking tourist they somehow feel their
symptoms increase. Doctors think the partial
understanding this allows, rather than the
complete lack of understanding if the group
were spouting Mandarin Chinese, for example,
can somehow exacerbate the symptoms (in much

the same way as an unavoidably overheard mobile-phone conversation on a train is said to be all the more annoying because you only hear one half of it). Sadly, many **rotathecaphobes** (q.v.) are wrongly diagnosed as **viatorphobes**; in a recent case, a London office worker tried to throw three separate groups of Japanese folk into the Thames before his true condition was diagnosed.

[orig. der.: *viator*, traveller; *dux*, chief]

◄O►

viciquinquiphobia
fear of Christmas

Children might refuse to believe in **viciquinqui-phobia** in the same way they cannot understand there being folk who don't like Skittles. **Viciquinquiphobes** are on the increase. They fear several things, from the commercialisation of the season to its prematurity (it is now possible to buy Christmas decorations whilst on your summer holiday). Others fear the general palaver, the compulsion to be with family (possible **pro-riophobes**, q.v.) and the irrational desire to drink advocaat. Sadly, some fear the loneliness, while others fear the company; some fear the ridiculous amount of money they will spend, others the fact that they have no money *to* spend. Only children are immune, it seems. The word, incidentally, has its origins in the Latin were for 'twenty-five', and didn't come into common usage until Charles Dickens had Scrooge say it in his classic, *A Christmas Carol*, with the line, '"Bah! Humbug," said Scrooge, "Christmas, be jiggered. The sooner every man jack in this world's a viciquinquiphobe, the better!"'

[orig. der.: *viceni*, twenty; *quinque*, five]

virgophobia
fear of being left on the shelf

A pheromone study conducted in the late 1990s by the University of Twickenham (formerly Eel Pie Island Poly) resulted in one surprising and, to be fair, not particularly useful conclusion: you can smell desperation. This is bad news for **virgophobes**, who, generally, are trying so hard they are almost levitating. **Virgophobia** can strike at any age, but the sight of a menacing, neon-flashing '40 YEARS' sign in the rear-view mirror tends to be the catalyst for most sufferers. This leads to the ironic but not altogether useless situation whereby psychiatrists' waiting rooms across the country are very often the best place to meet like-minded, late-thirty-something **virgophobes**. True **virgophobes** know that they have to take their foot off the gas, so to speak, if they are not to appear desperate, but that is easier said than done. It's like being surrounded by a pack of underfed Dobermanns while wearing a suit made of pork, with someone saying, 'Now, don't show them you're scared.' **Virgophobes** must keep telling themselves not to worry: it will happen when they least expect it. And that's true. I know one woman who was *definitely* not expecting it. Not at eighty-seven.

[orig. der.: *virgo*, virgin]

vilimusophobia
fear of lift music

Until recently, this phobia was thought to be merely a minority affair, with not more than a handful of sufferers. Now, however, thanks to the pioneering work of the late Spike Milligan – who was said to have once ripped a speaker from its wall mount because it was playing such offensive background music – we now realise that a huge proportion of the population suffer from **vilimusophobia**. The only problem is getting accurate numbers as, due to the very nature of this hidden, background music, most people do not know they are suffering. **Vilimusophobia,** which is more accurately thought of as fear of muzak or fear of background music (there was a time when it was confusingly referred to as 'piped music'), very often tricks the sufferer. They know something is wrong but they just can't put their finger on it. Most often, they think they can *smell* something odd. Those that get beyond this first stage and realise that it is the latent music they fear – commonly iPod users and hotel workers – mostly display year-round frowns and tend to give the evil eye to wall-mounted speakers in public places. Often **vilimusophobia** afflicts civil liberties campaigners and goes hand in hand with a passionate hatred of the increasingly ubiquitous CCTV camera.

[orig. der.: *vilis*, worthless; *musicus*, music]

—◈—

vilitasophobia
fear of being in the bargain clearance area

To give this phobia its full definition a little space and a prevailing wind are required: it is actually *the fear that being in a bargain clearance area will somehow make you believe you need the produce therein*. You can see why it gets abbreviated (the phobia that dare not speak its kennel name). A **vilitasophobe** will remember the feeling, from their pre-phobia days. There they are, on the furniture warehouse front line, ready to engage, enemy check-outs on the horizon. Suddenly, through no fault of their own, they find themselves wandering through the clearance section of the store. Items which seemed like tat only feet away in their rightful section have, here, the allure of long-lost Minoan treasure. On a bad day, they buy until they feel dirty. On a good day, they run like a goose. This is the predicament of the **vilitasophobe** – would you want to be cured for this? A world where the word 'reduced' translates as 'of immeasurable value'; 'bargain' makes them lean their heads to one side, smile and say 'Aw' pathetically, eyes alight as if they have just seen a member of the opposite sex who is out of their league. Oddly enough, in this world, the logic doesn't work backwards. That is, items which are *more* expensive than normal are as appealing, if not more, than cheap items. It's called the catch-19.99 (reduced from 22).

[orig. der.: *vilitas*, worthlessness]

◄◊►

visulibophobia
fear of seeing the film of a book

Visulibophobia is a twin-headed beast, of which **visulibophobia dilecta** is by far the most common form. The *v.d.* (1) sufferer fears seeing the film of their *favourite* book. It's not so much a phobia, more a character flaw. No cinematic representation of their *libris mirabilis* would be good enough, even if it had Robert Altman directing, Quentin Tarantino on grip and Kurosawa as best boy. Thus **visulibophobes** resist trailing off to see the movie at all, preferring to live with their fears by endlessly telling you how the book 'really does reward the re-reader'. *Visulibophobia diversa* sufferers, on the other hand, tend to be able to make the leap and go and see the film of the book, generally because it is not necessarily their favourite. Sufferers of *v.d.* (2) fear 'the change': the changes made to the book, that is. They are unable to understand why a director spends millions buying the rights to a certain story if they then fundamentally change it. 'Why not write their own story?' they think. They nevertheless tend to be able to overcome their phobia for periods of around 120–180 minutes – just long enough to see the film. From this moment on, they appear to commence every sentence with the phrase, 'And what were they thinking of by . . .' as they list another of the many heinous crimes against literature that the director has committed. Other offshoots of the generic phobia are **visiteraphobia,** in which sufferers fear seeing a *remake* of a favourite movie, and **visiproxophobia,** where the patient fears any movie bearing a *number* after the title (sometimes known as Saxosus syndrome). Therapists specialising in these phobias were recently to be seen demonstrating outside the premiere of *The Producers*, arguing that a musical film remake of a musical play of a non-musical original film could set their members back years.

[orig. der.: *visus*, vision; *liber*, book; *dilectus*, favourite; *diversus*, different; *iterum*, again; *proximus*, next; *saxosus*, rocky]

Index

Acknowledgements

To Emily Sweet for making this *so* much better. To Chiki Sarker (best of luck), Rosemary Davidson, Mary Davis, Kate Bland and all the team at Bloomsbury for their enthusiasm and hard work. To Jon Stock for taking this thing on at the *Daily Telegraph* in the first place. To Jim Smith for his fantastic artwork. To Simon Bates for his endless help and encouragement. To Gareth Davies for his guidance. To Darren, Giles, Annie, Charlotte, Emma and all the team at Classic FM for their forbearance. To Penny and Bob for getting us through the year. To Mum and Gerard for all their help and support. And, of course, to Millie, Daisy and Finn for just being Millie, Daisy and Finn, and for putting up with 'Daddy in the den' all the time.

A NOTE ON THE AUTHOR

Tim Lihoreau is a fronsophobic hebdomophobe, born in Leeds in 1965. Following early holusophobia, he studied music at Leeds University, where the first signs of his caerulophobia became apparent. After his manepostophobic graduation, he played the piano for a living, only overcoming his officinophobia in 1990, when he started at Jazz FM.

In 1991, he conquered uxorphobia to marry Siobhan, before moving to work at Classic FM in 1993, where, it is thought, the first symptoms of primaforaphobia led him to gain the rank of Creative Director. He is the author of several books – he notably overcame cadophobia to write *The Incomplete and Utter History of Classical Music* with Stephen Fry – and is a contributor to both the *Daily Telegraph* and the *Independent*, something which helps his disabling contumaphobia. He is a calvophobic arcaphobe with excirculophobic tendencies, who, by way of therapy for his ceterinfanophobia, now lives in Cambridge with his wife and their three children.

A NOTE ON THE TYPE

The text of this book is set in Linotype Sabon, named after the type founder, Jacques Sabon. It was designed by Jan Tschichold and jointly developed by Linotype, Monotype, and Stempel, in response to a need for a typeface to be available in identical form for mechanical hot metal composition and hand composition using foundry type. Tschichold based his design for Sabon roman on a font engraved by Garamond, and Sabon italic on a font by Granjon. It was first used in 1966 and has proved an enduring modern classic.